A Look Inside

A Look Inside

*Sonnets, Quatrains, Pantoums
and Other Poems*

G. H. Paulson

A Look Inside
Sonnets, Quatrains, Pantoums and Other Poems
G. H. Paulson

Copyright © 2024 G. H. Paulson
All rights reserved
ISBN: 9798329896213

No part of this book may be reproduced, or stored in a retrieval system, or transmitted in any form or by any means, electronic, mechanical, photocopying, recording, or otherwise, without express written permission of the publisher.

No part of this book may be used for AI machine learning.

Published by COZY CAT CREATIVE

Table of Contents

INTRODUCTION
1

SONNET
5

PANTOUM
21

FREE VERSE
31

VILLANELLE
53

ANAPODOTON
59

HAIKU
63

LIMERICK
83

CHOKA
91

ROUNDABOUT
95

TRINET
99

TRILONNET
105

QUATRAIN
109

RHYMING COUPLET
177

ACKNOWLEDGEMENT
183

INTRODUCTION

    To me, writing poems is like solving puzzles, as well as a way to express thoughts and opinions. Various styles of poetry have specific qualities to follow in their creation, which requires fitting together words, syllables, number of lines, and rhythm, like puzzle pieces. This collection of original poems contains several styles with an explanation of format for each. I encourage readers to try writing their own material following the basic guidelines, and have fun "solving" their own puzzles, while also telling a story or describing a moment in time. As evidenced by my poems, you can write from your own personal point of view, or imagine being someone or something else, and wondering how they think or feel. This is not a textbook. It is a reference point to get you thinking. Use these puzzles as a guide, not as rules to box in your creativity.

Most importantly, write, write, write.

FOREVER WORDS

THESE WORDS ARE MINE AND MINE ALONE
WRIT HERE ON PAPER, NOT CAST IN STONE
A PIECE OF ME TO LIVE ON ITS OWN
WHEN I AM JUST SOME DIRT AND BONE

UNIQUE, MY OWN, ONE OF A KIND
WORDS FROM SOMEWHERE DEEP IN MY MIND
THEY MAY NOT BE USEFUL, FUN, OR PROFOUND
TO YOU, BUT TO ME THEY ARE CERTAINLY SOUND

WORDS THAT APPEARED FROM I DON'T KNOW WHERE
JUMBLED AND SCRAMBLED AND TOSSED IN THE AIR
WORDS THAT I GRAB, PICK, PLACE, AND POST
IN AN ORDER I FEEL IS NEEDED THE MOST

AT SOME POINT I THINK I'VE DONE THE LAST QUOTE
PUT DOWN PEN AND PAPER TO SEE WHAT I WROTE
THE VERY BEST PART OF THIS CLEVER ENDEAVOR
IS WHERE I HAVE AN END DATE,
THESE WORDS LIVE FOREVER

SONNET

Derived from the word "sonetto" which means "little song," a sonnet takes on various forms. The most widely known form became famous from the writings of William Shakespeare. This form has 14 lines, consisting of three groups of four lines (a quatrain), and one last group of two lines (a couplet). Typically, each line has ten syllables. There is a pattern to the rhyme - the first line rhyming with the third line and the second line rhyming with the fourth line - in each quatrain. This is identified as an ABAB pattern in the first quatrain, CDCD in the second, EFEF in the third, and GG in the final couplet. Another type of sonnet, the curtal sonnet, contains ten lines, with ten syllables per line, and a final line of two stressed syllables. In the beginning, most sonnets were written with themes of love or emotion. In more modern times they are written about all sorts of subjects. Variations of sonnets may have less than 14 lines, no rhyming pattern or different rhyming patterns, and may have more than ten syllables per line - typically, the number of syllables per line remains consistent throughout the piece, although, you will see variations on this as well.

WHAT IS LIFE

SUCH SOUNDS CAN SOOTHE THE MINDS OF SAVAGE MEN
INSPIRE A DREAMER FAR BEYOND A DREAM
MAKE OLD TIRED BODIES RISE AND THINK OF WHEN
THEY DANCED TIL DAWN AND ON EACH OTHER LEANED

FROM RUMBLING LOW TO PLUNKING WAY UP HIGH
AN ENDLESS MIX OF MOODS ARE NEATLY MADE
BY DIGITS DANCING SWIFTLY BY AND BY
ALLOWING LIFE'S SWEET VISIONS TO PERSUADE

THESE MOMENTS ARE THE KIND I HOLD SO DEAR
TO RECREATE A FEELING I HAVE KNOWN
SO WELL THAT YOU CAN SEE IT WITH YOUR EAR
AND KNOW WHAT I HAVE FELT AS I HAVE GROWN

I KNOW IT MIGHT BE HARD TO UNDERSTAND
BUT WHAT IS LIFE WITHOUT A BABY GRAND

TRUTH BE TOLD

I PRACTICED MY LINES ALL MY LIFE,
FOR MANY MULTIFACETED SCENES
PREPARED MENTALLY FOR THE STRIFE,
OF FULFILLING MULTIPLE DREAMS

SO MANY SIMPLE INCIDENTS,
TOGETHER CREATED MY STORY,
HYPNOTIZED AND BAPTIZED I WENT,
OUT IN THE WORLD TO SEEK GLORY

I MET PEOPLE, PEOPLE MET ME,
WE ALL SHARED WHO WE THOUGHT WE WERE
MANY MECHANISTIC TRUTHS BECAME,
OUR LIVES GOING BY IN A BLUR

SO FAST; WE NEVER TOOK A LOOK,
TO SEE US AS COVERS, NOT BOOKS

SONETTO

SOMETIMES I WANT TO SIMPLY SING A LOVELY LITTLE SONG

SEND VIBRATIONS THROUGH THE AIR FOR EVERY EAR TO HEAR

SOUNDS SOFT AND SOOTHING DRAWING OTHERS CLOSE TO SING ALONG

A MIXING POT OF BASS AND TREBLE, FALSETTOS WITHOUT FEAR

JUST A LITTLE MELODY, CALMING IN SIMPLICITY

CLOSE YOUR EYES AND PICTURE PEACE, SIMPLE SCENES SERENE

TWO DOVES COOING ON A BRANCH, HIGH UP IN A TREE

WIND CHIMES SOFTLY TOUCHING, BIRTHING SOUNDS SUBLIME

SOMETIMES I WANT TO SIMPLY SING A LOVELY LITTLE SONG

YET, I'M QUITE AFRAID THE ADVENTURE WILL SURELY TURN OUT POOR

AS I HAVE SUNG ALL ALONE, AND IT ALWAYS SOUNDS SO WRONG

EVERYONE WOULD FLEE, NOT GATHER ROUND, OF THAT I'M VERY SURE

SO, WHEN I DESIRE TO SING A LOVELY LITTLE SIMPLE TUNE

I LOOK FOR PEN AND PAPER TO START WRITING IN MY ROOM

LONELY ROAD

FAR DOWN MY LONELY ROAD, I SEE A FIGURE COMING SLOW
A TINY DARKENED DOT, GROWING TALL WITH EACH FORWARD MOVE
SHUFFLING ALONG, INEXORABLY HE WOULD GO
COMMITTED TO A GRUELING PATH, TO HIMSELF HE HAD TO PROVE

WHITE AND SILVER STRANDS SCATTERED BELOW HIS WOOLY HAT
A STOIC GAZE, A STEADY GAIT, A MOVEMENT TOWARDS A GOAL
HIS DARK ATTIRE DRAPED TO THE GROUND, IT WAS A WONDER THAT
HE TRAVELED HERE, WITH NO FEAR, NO CONCERN FOR WHAT THE TOLL

LEANING ON HIS TUBES AND WHEELS, HANDS GRIPPED TIGHT AND STEADY
HE GLANCED AT ME, A NOD HELLO, HELLO I SEE YOU THERE
A QUIET HELLO, A MESSAGE PASSED? SOMEDAY I HOPE YOU'RE READY
TO SUMMON STRENGTH, TO RAISE RESOLVE, TO MAKE YOUR BODY CARE

AT THE INTERSECT A STEEP INCLINE, A CHOICE TO MAKE, UP OR DOWN
HE LOOKED LEFT, THEN UP, THEN RIGHT, THEN DOWN, THEN SLOWLY TURNED AROUND

TWO CITIES

TWO CITIES DISAPPEARED FROM OUR SHARED EARTH
THREE DAYS APART THEY VANISHED, VAPORIZED
CHILDREN WITH THEIR PETS, MOTHERS GIVING BIRTH
GONE BECAUSE SOMEONE THOUGHT THEY'D SAVE SOME LIVES?

THE SHOCK WAVE FLATTENED ALL THAT STOOD AROUND
SENT SHATTERED GLASS LIKE DAGGERS DOWN THE STREET
SURVIVORS RAN THROUGH BLOOD UPON THE GROUND
FROM SHARDS OF GLASS EMBEDDED IN THEIR MEAT

ERASED LIKE CHALK ON A SCHOOL BLACKBOARD
WERE DOCTORS, LAWYERS, SCIENTISTS, AND PRIESTS
THEIR VALUE TO HUMANITY IGNORED
BY FRIGHTENED MINDS REACTING LIKE WILD BEASTS

NOW WE SIT HERE FOREVER WITH THE FEAR
THAT ONE FINAL TIME HORROR REAPPEARS

MORE?

WE HAVE ABUNDANCE IN OUR STORES,
SO MANY CHOICES, SO HARD TO CHOOSE
AISLES AND AISLES CONTAIN MORE AND MORE,
OF ITEMS WE DON'T NEED, BUT WHO'S

TO SAY WE SHOULD EVER DO WITH LESS,
TO REHEAT, NOT TO THROW AWAY
THESE PEOPLE CAN BE SUCH A PEST,
I'LL DO IT MY WAY EVERY DAY

YES, ALL I EVER CARE TO SEE,
IS ALL ABUNDANCE ON DISPLAY
I SQUASH DOWN DEEP INSIDE OF ME,
A TRUTH I NEVER WANT TO SAY;

SOMEWHERE, SOMEONE'S SON OR DAUGHTER,
WAITS AND WAITS FOR BREAD OR WATER

CRITIQUE

FROM NOTHING THIS CREATION CAME TO FORM
NOT TO SEEK FORTUNE OR SOME FLEETING FAME
ARRIVAL DIDN'T FOLLOW ANY NORM
ANOTHER MYSTERY FROM WHENCE IT CAME

THE PROCESS DID NOT HAPPEN OVERNIGHT
YES, GHOSTLY VOICES CAME AND LEFT THEIR MARK
AND WAKING HOURS WERE SPENT TIL WANING LIGHT
ALL COMBINED TO GUIDE THE FIRE FROM THE SPARK

NOW FINALLY TO SEE THIS WORK COMPLETE
TO LEAVE THE ARDUOUS PATH FAR BEHIND
GET TO SEE THIS WORK STANDING SO REPLETE
SATISFACTION AND SUCCESS FILL MY MIND

AT LEAST THAT'S WHAT I FEEL FOR A SHORT TIME
THEN CREEPING CRITICISM STARTS ITS CLIMB

THE SCULPTOR

EVERY HOUR TO COME IS REDUNDANT
EVERY DAY MIRRORS MY HISTORY
I TRIED BEING MUCH DIFFERENT AND CAN'T
MY LIFE IS QUITE FAR FROM A MYSTERY

EACH BLOW FROM MY HAND RELEASES A CHIP
EVENTUALLY YOU WILL SEE WHAT I SEE
I AM STANDING ALL DAY IN MY RUBBLE
MEANINGLESS MARBLE THAT I HAVE SET FREE

THE VISION IN MY MEMORY MUST STAY
FIXED, FIRMLY PROJECTED BEFORE MY HANDS
THIS TIME THE VISION IS ME AND WON'T STRAY
SINCE SO SIMPLY I HAVE NO OTHER PLANS

WHEN ALL IS DONE YOU WILL SEE ME ALONE
WITH A HAND REACHING OUT FROM SOLID STONE

SOCRATES

ASK ANYONE ANYWHERE WHO IS SOCRATES
AND HERE IS WHAT THEY ARE LIKELY TO SAY
LIKE HIS FRIENDS SPARTACUS AND EUPHRATES
HE WAS A SPECIAL GENIUS IN HIS DAY

DIG DOWN A LITTLE DEEPER YET AND ASK
WERE HIS STUDENTS' GOALS AND HIS IN SYNCH
HE DIDN'T WANT DISCIPLES OR DUPLICATES
HE'D RATHER HAVE YOU THINK AND THINK AND THINK

UNTIL YOUR MIND IS FREE OF ARGUMENTS
THAT ONLY MAKE SENSE BECAUSE THEY ARE OLD
ALL OFFICIALS SAW AN ALTRUISTIC FOOL
THEY EXECUTED HIM AND LEFT HIM COLD

OFFICIALS STILL STAY STUCK IN SERVITUDE
WHILE SOPHIST WORDS REMAIN WORDS TO EXCLUDE

HOWLING WIND

A HOWLING WIND BLOWS IN THE DOOR
DISTURBING WHAT WAS THERE BEFORE
A SCREECHING, TWISTED, DISSONANCE
THAT TURNS SUCH PEACE INTO A WAR

A PRESENCE OF A CHILLING COLD
ENVELOPS ALL BOTH YOUNG AND OLD
IT HAS NO MOTIVE OR REGRETS
THIS HOWLING WIND THAT TAKES A TOLL

IT SOUNDS LIKE FOOTSTEPS IN THE HALL
STACCATO CLICK CLACKS FOR US ALL
NOT WARNINGS BUT AN ARROGANCE
A PEACOCK STRUT, COYOTE CALL

THANK GOD FOR TIME, AS THIS WON'T LAST
THE FUTURE WILL NOT BE THE PAST

CLOSURE

IT WAS NOT HIS MISTAKE HOW HE APPEARED
IT WASN'T HIS FAULT WHERE HIS PARENTS RESIDE
IT WASN'T HIS WISH TO BE HATED OR FEARED
WHO SAID OKAY STREET JUSTICE BE APPLIED

MULTIPLE RACES CAN ALL LOOK AWAY
OR JOIN THE CROWD TO TEACH THIS MAN RULES
VIDEO SHOWED HIS LIFE DRAINING AWAY
LYING THERE BENEATH THE TOWERS OF BLUE

A SON IS LOST AND A FATHER IS TOO
DO NOT TELL ME CLOSURE HEALS MY LOST SOUL
DON'T SAY IT TO HIS NIECE OR HIS NEPHEW
DON'T EVEN THINK CLOSURE HEALS THE HEART'S HOLE

THROW CLOSURE OUT OF THE BOOK OF WORDS
WITHOUT RESURRECTION THE THOUGHT IS ABSURD

PLATO'S SONGS

OH YES, THE TIMES WERE CHANGIN' WAY BACK THEN
BOB'S WICKED WORDS WERE BURNING IN OUR SOUL
WE THOUGHT, WE SHOUTED, MARCHED AND HOPED FOR WHEN
AN END TO HATE WOULD STOP A DEATHLY TOLL

IMAGINE A NEW POSSIBILITY
JOHN ASKED US FOR VISION OUTSIDE THE BOX
YES, ALL THE PEOPLE WITH HIS SAME FANTASY
COULD MAKE IT REAL AND SEE WHAT IT UNLOCKS

GRATITUDE AND MY BODY ARE DISTINCT
ANI'S SOULFUL SONG SPOKE A SOLID TRUTH
BEFORE MEN ACT THEY NEED TO THINK
WILL WHAT I DO BE SEEN AS QUITE UNCOUTH

WHOSE SEARING SONGS ARE SINGING FOR US NOW
IT SEEMS SILENCE OVERTOOK US ALL SOMEHOW

BOSS

A BOSS CAN GUIDE YOU TO MUCH HIGHER HEIGHTS
THROUGH EDUCATED ENABLING EYES
THAT RECALL YEARS OF CRASHES AND FLIGHTS
REVEALING GEMS THAT OFTEN EXPLAIN WHY

SOME SIMPLE METHODS SIMPLY WORK THE BEST
COMPLICATED CONCERNS CAN CONFUSE
KEEP IT SIMPLE STUPID "KISS" KILLS THE REST
AN ACRONYM TO WIN NOT TO LOSE

WE ALL HAVE URGES TO REINVENT A WHEEL
USE OUR YOUTHFUL ENERGY TRAPPED WITHIN
THINK OUTSIDE A BOX BUILT OF ELDER STEEL
TO HOLD US BACK WOULD BE A MORTAL SIN

BUT BOSSES BUY US TIME TO GET IT RIGHT
THEY ONCE WERE US AND NOW THEY SHINE THE LIGHT

NO JUDGEMENT

THE MONARCH MOVES IN RANDOM SCATTERED WAYS
NO BUSY BEELINE TO FLOWERS HAPPENING HERE
SUCH ERRATIC MOVES KEEP ME FEELING TENSE
FROM TREE TO BUSH TO FLOWERS SHE PLAYS
IT SEEMS LIKE THERE EXISTS NO WAY TO STEER
A RANDOM ILLUSION FOR ITS DEFENSE?
BUT WITH ALL THE UPS, DOWNS, LEFTS, RIGHTS, AND DELAY
THE BUTTERFLY MAKES IT VERY, VERY CLEAR
SHE'LL GO HER WAY, I SHOULD NOT TAKE OFFENSE
I SHOULD JUST WATCH, ENJOY, GO ON MY WAY
MAKE SENSE?

PANTOUM

Originally a Malaysian writing used by minstrels traveling the countryside, the pantoum has become more popular in recent years. A pantoum consists of quatrains, or four-line stanzas, in which the second and fourth lines of each quatrain are duplicated, word for word, as the first and third lines of the next quatrain. These can be any number of quatrains in length. The last line of the poem is often the same as the first line of the poem. The rhyme pattern can be ABAB, or no rhyme at all.

REFLECTIONS

I WATCHED YOUR SMILE IN THE WINDOW
WE SAT TOGETHER ON THE TRAIN
THE REFLECTION MESMERIZING
NOT REAL, BUT JUST THE SAME

WE SAT TOGETHER ON THE TRAIN
I LOOKED OUT AND SAW YOUR FACE
NOT REAL, BUT JUST THE SAME
FLOATING OVER TREES AND SHRUBS ALONG THE WAY

I LOOKED OUT AND SAW YOUR FACE
AN ANGELIC APPARITION
FLOATING OVER TREES AND SHRUBS ALONG THE WAY
I HOPED THE TRAIN DIDN'T STOP BEFORE I HAD A NAME

AN ANGELIC APPARITION
BEGAN TO SLOWLY FADE AWAY
I HOPED THE TRAIN DIDN'T STOP BEFORE I HAD A NAME
MY FATE THAT DAY, HESITATION ONCE AGAIN

A GUPPY MOM

A GUPPY MOM GIVES BIRTH TO NINE
THEY SWIM OFF AND SURVIVE
MOST OF THEM WILL DO REAL WELL
UNTIL A PREDATOR ARRIVES

THEY SWIM OFF AND SURVIVE
KNOWING WHAT TO DO
UNTIL A PREDATOR ARRIVES
FROM A SURVIVAL POINT OF VIEW

KNOWING WHAT TO DO
IS IT LEARNED OR DNA
FROM A SURVIVAL POINT OF VIEW
IT DEPENDS ON WHO'S AT PLAY

IS IT LEARNED OR DNA
THIS ABILITY TO HOPE
IT DEPENDS ON WHAT'S AT PLAY
HUMANS NEED EIGHTEEN YEARS TO COPE

THIS ABILITY TO HOPE
FOR HUMANS REALLY TOUGH
HUMANS NEED EIGHTEEN YEARS TO COPE
WE NURTURE, TEACH, PLAY ROUGH

FOR HUMANS REALLY TOUGH
AND WE DON'T MAKE IT EVERY TIME
WE NURTURE, TEACH, PLAY ROUGH
A GUPPY MOM GIVES BIRTH TO NINE

CHOICE

DID THEY CHOOSE TO HAVE NO CHOICE
TO LIVE BENEATH A BRIDGE
TO HIKE THE RAILROAD TRACK
NEVER EATING FROM A FRIDGE

TO LIVE BENEATH A BRIDGE
WITHOUT A SHOWER OR A BOWL
NEVER EATING FROM A FRIDGE
MUST TAKE AN AWFUL TOLL

WITHOUT A SHOWER OR A BOWL
WITHOUT A SAFE WINDOWED ROOM
MUST TAKE AN AWFUL TOLL
AND CONJURE UP SOME DOOM

WITHOUT A SAFE WINDOWED ROOM
THE WOUNDED SCREAMS SOUND OUT
AND CONJURE UP SOME DOOM
MAKING SANITY A DOUBT

THE WOUNDED SCREAMS SOUND OUT
THE DRUGS DON'T EASE THE FRIGHT
MAKING SANITY A DOUBT
MAKING SLEEP A LOSS AT NIGHT

THE DRUGS DON'T EASE THE FRIGHT
FRIGHT PILES ON THE PAIN
MAKING SLEEP A LOSS AT NIGHT
PARANOIA STARTS TO GAIN

FRIGHT PILES ON THE PAIN
ON THIS GROUP WITHOUT A VOICE
PARANOIA STARTS TO GAIN
DO THEY CHOOSE TO HAVE NO CHOICE

FROM THE CORNERS OF MY MIND

A RESOLUTION'S NOT EFFECTIVE
UNLESS YOU REMEMBER WHAT IT WAS
AT THE AGE THAT I AM GETTING
MY MIND DOES WHAT IT DOES

UNLESS YOU REMEMBER WHAT IT WAS
WHAT'S THE POINT TO STAKE A CLAIM
MY MIND DOES WHAT IT DOES
AND IT'S NOT ALWAYS THE SAME

WHAT'S THE POINT TO STAKE A CLAIM
WHEN YOUR MEMORY'S A SIEVE
AND IT'S NOT ALWAYS THE SAME
YES, IT SOMETIMES DOESN'T GIVE

WHEN YOUR MEMORY'S A SIEVE
A RESOLUTION'S NOT THE WAY
YES, IT SOMETIMES DOESN'T GIVE
WHAT WAS I GOING TO SAY?

THE SHACK

MOM WAS OUTSIDE CHOPPING SUGARCANE
THE DOCTOR LIVED SO MANY MILES AWAY
MY ONLY CHOICE WAS LIE THERE IN MY SWEAT
EVEN IF WE WALKED, WE HAD NO WAY TO PAY

THE DOCTOR LIVED SO MANY MILES AWAY
A LUXURY FOR THOSE WHO HAD A BIKE
EVEN IF WE WALKED, WE HAD NO WAY TO PAY
LIFE HERE'S NOT ABOUT WHAT I WOULD LIKE

A LUXURY FOR THOSE WHO HAD A BIKE
TO SEE A WORLD FAR BEYOND THE FIELD
LIFE HERE'S NOT ABOUT WHAT I WOULD LIKE
IT'S ABOUT THE LACK OF POWER THAT I WIELD

TO SEE A WORLD FAR BEYOND THE FIELD
A FOOLISH FEVERED DREAM I'D NOT ATTAIN
IT'S ABOUT THE LACK OF POWER THAT I WIELD
MOM WAS OUTSIDE CHOPPING SUGARCANE

MIND TO BODY

OH THE WASTED EARLY YEARS
THE CIGARETTES AND BOOZE
I SURELY KNEW THE CONSEQUENCE
I DIDN'T THINK I'D LOSE

THE CIGARETTES AND BOOZE
HOW COULD I GROW UP STRONG
I DIDN'T THINK I'D LOSE
SIRENS SAY I'M WRONG

HOW COULD I GROW UP STRONG
HAVE VIBRANT SKIN AND BONE
SIRENS SAY I'M WRONG
I TRY NOW TO ATONE

HAVE VIBRANT SKIN AND BONE
WITH ORGANS WORKING FINE
I TRY NOW TO ATONE
TOO LATE I THINK THIS TIME

WITH ORGANS WORKING FINE
I WOULDN'T NEED THIS RIDE
TOO LATE I THINK THIS TIME
THEY'RE WHEELING ME INSIDE

WE WOULDN'T NEED THIS RIDE
IF I HAD THOUGHT OF US AS PEERS
THEY'RE WHEELING US INSIDE
OH THE WASTED EARLY YEARS

FREE VERSE

Any form of poetry that does not necessarily rhyme, or follow any specific pattern, is known as free verse. This is similar to how we naturally speak.

BEYOND

HE RAN THROUGH THE FIELD WITH ABANDON
FLAILING ARMS, HIGH PITCHED VOICE
HE SUDDENLY PAUSED
THEN TOOK OFF SPRINTING FURIOUSLY
TRIPPING, HE ROLLED DOWN A HILL
STOPPING WITH ARMS AND LEGS
STRETCHED OUT IN AN X
HE GAZED UP AT WHITE BILLOWY CLOUDS
PERCHED ON THE MOUNTAINTOP
SILENT AND STILL
HE NOTICED THE SKY BEGAN
AT THE FIELD'S EDGES
THEN ROSE OVERHEAD AND STOPPED
AT THE MOUNTAIN PEAK
HE THOUGHT HE WAS LYING INSIDE
HALF A BALL
PAINTED WITH BLUES AND BROWNS AND WHITES
HE WONDERED WHAT EXISTED
ON THE OTHER SIDE

FADE AWAY

SUNLIGHT PEERING THROUGH GREEN TINTED PANES DOES NOT TEACH DILATED PUPILS IN A PROPER COLLEGE MANNER

AS THE MIND IS BLOWN INTO CONCENTRIC CIRCLES OF ANIMATED LIFE FRAMED BY MAN'S BIRTH AND DEATH

COLLISIONS OF MIND AND BODY CAUSED BY IRREPRESSIBLE FEAR, ANXIETY, LOVE, AND SORROW, CRUSH THE THOUGHTS OF MAN IN HIS CAGE

REVEALING LIFE AS A SNOWBALL ROLLING DOWNHILL GAINING BOTH SIZE AND MOMENTUM BEFORE COLLISION WITH AN IMMOVABLE STONE

AWAKE
FLY FREE TO A TERPSICHOREAN WORLD, BE A DEER DARTING THROUGH DAISIES, HAVING NO LOVER, LOVING NO HAVING, NO TEARS TO FALL IN THE POLLEN
AWAKE
LEAVE THIS DOORLESS ROOM
AWAKE
BREAK FREE FROM THIS CHRYSALIS TOMB
AWAKE, FLY FREE
AND FADE AWAY INTO FREEDOM

THE LAST SONG

THIS PIANO
TWISTS OF STEEL
MITERED WOOD
STANDING SILENT
AMIDST THE RUBBLE
OF MY APATHY

DRESSED IN HER DARK BLACK COAT
WAITING
PATIENTLY
TEMPTING MY HAND
TO TOUCH HER
ONE MORE TIME

MY FRIEND, FOR YOU
TOMORROW IS ANOTHER DAY
TIME, MY FRIEND
TO SOUND THE THOUGHT
OF SOME NEW STRANGER

WHILE I TRAVEL TO THE PLACE
I CAME FROM
OVER ROADS
THAT I FORGOT

MY TIRED BODY
SUBSCRIBES NO MORE
TO URGES
OF MY MIND
NO LONGER CAN I MAKE YOU SING
AND WARM THIS MIDNIGHT AIR

CORE OF MY LIFE!
IMMUTABLE
YOU STAND BEFORE ME
A GRANITE SHORE
CARESSED
BY TIME'S PONDEROUS WAVES

WAVES THAT HAVE WEAKENED ME
MY DEAREST FRIEND
NOW, ALL I HAVE TO LEAVE
FOR YOU….
IS THIS ACAPELLA SONG

THE TURN

WHEN TREES TURN INTO GRAPHITE LINES
AGAINST DREARY GRAYISH SKIES
AND WEIGHT BUILDS ON BODIES
TO PUSH THEM DOWN IN LEAVES
IT'S HARD TO KEEP FROM GOING UNDER
TO FIND MOTIVATION
TO SURVIVE
WHEN TREES TURN INTO GRAPHITE LINES
AGAINST DREARY GRAYISH SKIES

THE UNKNOWN OBSERVER

METEORLIKE SPOTS
SPEEDING ACROSS MY EYES
DISTANT SOUNDS
FROM NEARBY WALLS
WHAT A CLEVER DISGUISE
PEOPLE STARING AT ME
WHEN THEY DON'T KNOW THAT THEY ARE
AND WORST OF ALL
THEY'RE WHISPERING
I'M CERTAIN
THAT THEY ARE
IF I COULD FIND THE PERSON
WHO'S DOING THIS TO ME
I WOULDN'T KNOW WHO I FOUND
NO LONGER WOULD HE BE

SLEEPY THOUGHTS

RED CANNA ON CONCRETE
MOTOR SCOOTER THROUGH A CROWD
POSTER ON A BACK
HELD WITH A RUBBER BAND
WHAT ABOUT NOW
THINKING WHAT ABOUT NOW
TOO LIGHT TO BE LATE
TOO DIM TO BE UP
THE ENEMY STILL LOSING?
CITIES STILL THERE
WHAT ABOUT NOW
THINKING WHAT ABOUT NOW
EYES OPEN EYES SHUT
DOESN'T MATTER AT ALL
ONE WAY IS REAL
THE OTHER A SCROLL
A HOODED FACE
I DON'T RECOGNIZE
TRAPPED IN A TRAILER
THE WATERS STILL RISE

THINKING WHAT ABOUT NOW
IS THIS THE MOMENT
THE IMAGES LEAVE
STORIES GO COLD
THE PCH SUITCASE
FADES AWAY
WHAT ABOUT NOW
THINKING WHAT ABOUT NOW
NOW CAN I REST?

A MOMENT

AS THE CLOCK TICKS,
I WALK THROUGH A ROSE GARDEN.
I CAN DESCRIBE THE COLORS, SMELLS,
THE SIZES AND SHAPES.
FOR A TIME;
THEN MY MEMORY,
FOLDS IN UPON ITSELF,
OVER AND OVER,
UNTIL I REMEMBER A GARDEN,
NOT A ROSE.
AS THE CLOCK TICKS,
I WALK THROUGH LIFE,
NOTICING COLORS, SIZES, SMELLS,
ATTITUDES,
BEHAVIORS.
AS THE CLOCK TICKS,
I MOSTLY REMEMBER A GARDEN,
EXCEPT,
FOR THAT PRESENCE,
INDESCRIBABLE, UNDEFINABLE, UNTELLABLE, UNTOUCHED,
BUT TRUE,
AND WARMING,
CONNECTED.

A DIFFERENT WORLD

HE WAS IN THE MIDDLE OF THE ROAD
SHOELESS, SHIRTLESS
COVERED IN GRAFFITI
PANTS COVERING ONE LEG
THE OTHER LEG BARE
INDEX FINGERS POINTED SKYWARD
SLOWLY, HE BENT AT THE WAIST
INDEX FINGERS POINTED DOWN
HIS BARE FEET DID BISCUITS ON THE PAVEMENT
LIKE A KITTEN AT HER MOTHER'S BELLY
HE COULD HAVE BEEN A STRAY DOG
HE WAS ONCE A MAN
CREATED EQUAL
NOW SEEN AS SO MUCH LESS
AN ANNOYANCE ON A PATH
A CROW DANCING IN THE ROAD

WHAT IF

WHAT WOULD BE DIFFERENT
IF YOU WERE WRONG
WHAT WOULD CHANGE
WHO WOULD NO LONGER AVOID YOU

WHAT COULD YOU HAVE ACCOMPLISHED
WHERE WOULD YOU BE
WHAT WOULD CHANGE
ARE YOU ABLE TO SEE

WOULD YOU SMILE AND SEE THE GOOD
NO LONGER BE ANNOYED
WHAT WOULD CHANGE
WHO WOULD YOU BE

WHAT DID YOU SACRIFICE
TO OWN YOUR OWN TRUTH
WHAT WOULD CHANGE
IF YOU COULD SEE

HOW FAR DOES THE STONE MOVE
WHEN PUSHED FROM BOTH SIDES
WHAT WOULD CHANGE
DO YOU KNOW?

WHAT COULD BE DIFFERENT
IF YOU KNEW YOU WERE WRONG
CAN YOU CHANGE
BEFORE TIME STANDS STILL

PERHAPS

EVERY YEAR THE FLOWERS OF MAY
RISE UP
THEY SPEAK TO EACH OTHER
ALL COLORS JOYOUS
THEY HAVE RETURNED TOGETHER
AFTER NOURISHING SHOWERS
AND EARTH'S PRECIOUS NUTRIENTS
SPRING THEM TO LIFE
THEY DANCE IN THE WIND
SOAK IN THE SUN
CURL UP AND SLEEP AT NIGHT
CONFIDENT TOMORROW WILL COME—
SOFT RAIN BEFORE MAY CARESSES THE FLOWERS
AWAKENS THE PRIOR YEAR
GENTLY SOAKS ROOTS AND SPIRITS
ALLOWING FOR TRANQUILITY
SEEDS SCATTER FAR AWAY
TO SPREAD THEIR THOUGHTLESS BEAUTY
THESE LIVING WORKS OF ART
NOT KNOWING THAT THEY ARE

THE RAINS GROW HARDER EVERY YEAR
I FEAR THE FLOWERS SHOULD FEAR
MAY WILL COME AGAIN FOR SURE
AND AGAIN AND AGAIN AND AGAIN
BUT WILL THE FLOWERS HAVE A CHANCE
TO PROUDLY DO THEIR WIND SWEPT DANCE
OR WILL APRIL RAINS BE WHISTLING—
UNTIL SILENCE OVERWHELMS
PERHAPS AFTERWARDS
SOME ORPHANED SEEDS WILL FIND A HOME
PERHAPS TO START ANEW
PERHAPS

MUSTER

BLOSSOMS PEAK THROUGH THE MORNING MOUNTAIN HAZE
RANDOM SPLASHES OF PURITY
SCATTERED AMONG SHINY GREEN UNIFORMS
STRANDS OF STATELY STANDING STILTS
TALL AT ATTENTION
SILENTLY RADIATING PEACE TO PASSING EYES
AN AMAZING MAY MOMENT OF MEMORIAL GLORY
BURSTING FORTH WITH PURE WHITE PORCELAIN BEAUTIES
THE MAGNIFICENT MAGNOLIA

GREAT, GREAT, GRANDPA HAD A FEELING

GREAT, GREAT, GRANDPA
WOKE UP WITH A FEELING
SEARCHED HIS DARKENED ROOM
FOR HIS FAVORITE CHAIR
PULLED ON HIS BRITCHES
SEARCHED THE FLOOR FOR HIS BOOTS
STOOD UP AND FELT ALONG THE WALL
FOR HIS WOOL CAP
AND HUNTING JACKET
HE MADE IT TO THE FRONT DOOR
STEPPED OUT ON THE SPLINTERED DECK
GRABBED HIS RIFLE
STANDING AGAINST THE WALL
HE WARILY CAST HIS EYE AROUND
AS HE WALKED TO THE EDGE OF THE FOREST
HE PAUSED TO LISTEN FOR BEARS
THIS CLOUDY NIGHT, TOTAL SILENCE
HE LEANED HIS RIFLE
AGAINST A TREE
WAITED FOR THE RELIEVING SOUND
OF TINKLING ON THE LEAVES
THIS WAS HIS FIRST TRIP
OF A NIGHT OF THREE

TOWERING TREES

TOWERING TREES INTERTWINED LIMBS AND LEAVES
A CANOPY OF GREEN TO CAPTURE RAYS OF LIGHT
KEEPING LIFE BELOW IN DARKNESS.
TOWERING TREES INTERTWINE THEIR ROOTS
IN SEARCH OF NUTRIENTS AND WATER.
NEEDING MORE THAN LOWLY NEIGHBORS
COEXISTING, ONE TALL, DOMINANT AND OLD,
ONE WEAK, SMALL, AND FRAIL,
SURVIVING IN THE SHADOWS
COEXISTING, ONE SHINING IN THE SUN
ONE HIDDEN, OVERLOOKED BY EVERYONE.

TRUTH

I WAS TOLD A TRUTH TODAY
THAT BECAME MIXED IN
WITH MY HISTORY
WHAT CAME OUT TOOK SOME SUBTLE TURNS
SOME TWISTS SOME DIFFERENCE
BECAME SLIPPERY
I PASSED IT ALONG TO A FRIEND I KNEW
WHOSE OPINION WAS ADDED
INTO THE STEW
HE THEN TOLD ANOTHER
WHO ADDED THEIR THOUGHTS
THE TRUTH WAS WATERED
AND GREW AND GREW
NOW I WONDER IF THE TRUTH
ORIGINALLY TOLD
HAD GONE THROUGH THIS PROCESS
AND WAS REALLY QUITE OLD
NOT SOMETHING TRUE OR TRUTHFUL AT ALL
JUST ASSAILABLE THOUGHTS
A WATER FOUNDATION
FOR A CONCRETE WALL

GHOST WORDS

OPPRESSED PEOPLE FLED ACROSS A SEA
YEARNING TO BE FREE
TO START ANEW
IN A NEW WORLD
A LAND OF PROMISE ALREADY PROMISED
WHO KNEW
WHO CARED
WHO SHARED
JOINED BY OTHER HUDDLED MASSES
YEARNING TO BE FREE
THEY SPREAD OUT UNDER SPACIOUS SKIES
WITH THE AIM TO STAKE A CLAIM
UPON THIS FRUITED PLAIN
BOAT UPON BOAT BROUGHT HOPE TO THIS LAND
ALONG WITH THIEVES AND EVIL
AND IDEAS NOT SO GRAND
DEEP IN DARK HOLDS SHACKLED PEOPLE ARRIVED
TAKEN FROM FREEDOM TO TRY TO SURVIVE
ENDURING GREAT PAIN
WORKING FIELDS OF AMBER GRAIN
A COUNTRY WAS BORN
THEN BROKEN IN TWO

FIGHTING FOR JUSTICE
FOR THE DOWNTRODDEN FEW
THOUSANDS OF LIVES THAT SOUGHT FREEDOM WERE LOST
DEFENDING THE NOTION OF EQUALITY'S COST
TO COMMEMORATE THE END OF AN UNCIVIL WAR
FRANCE SENT A STATUE
TO GRACE NEW YORK'S SHORE
STANDING PROUDLY WITH BROKEN SHACKLES LAID AT HER FEET
LIFTING A LAMP FOR THE TIRED AND POOR
TO SEE THEIR WAY HERE FOR FREEDOM ONCE MORE
WE SING THE SONGS; RECITE THE WORDS
TRY TO STAY TRUE TO OUR FOREFATHERS' DREAMS
TO LIVE FREE AS ONE COUNTRY INVITING TO ALL
NOT TORN IN TWO BY THE GREED OF A FEW
WHO BUILD WALLS AND FENCES LIKE SYMBOLS OF HATE
NOT SOARING GRAND STATUES TO STAND AT OUR GATE

VILLANELLE

A villanelle is 19 lines long. It consists of five stanzas, with three lines each (a tercet), and a final stanza of four lines (a quatrain). This is the most complex puzzle to solve of all the styles shared in this book. I recommend reading some examples side by side with this definition so it doesn't get too jumbled. The first line of the first tercet will be the last line of the second and fourth tercets. The last line of the first tercet will be the last line of the third and fifth tercets. These two lines will also be the last two lines of the poem.

PERSPECTIVE

SOMEWHERE A PEACEFUL BLUE DOT EXISTS
WITH OCEANS, CLOUDS AND HARMONY
IT JUST DEPENDS ON WHERE ONE SITS

CRACKED RIVER BEDS, A TORNADO TWISTS
BARREN FIELDS, MONTHS OF NO RAIN
SOMEWHERE A PEACEFUL BLUE DOT EXISTS

SOLDIERS IN TRENCHES TAKING HITS
POLITICIANS COUNTING CASH
IT JUST DEPENDS ON WHERE ONE SITS

HATE FILLED SOULS ARE MAKING LONG LISTS
OF THOSE TO DENY, DENIGRATE
SOMEWHERE A PEACEFUL BLUE DOT EXISTS

OCEANS ARE FILLED WITH PLASTIC BITS
MOUNTAIN STREAMS STILL SEEM CLEAR AND COOL
IT JUST DEPENDS ON WHERE ONE SITS

MOVE AROUND AND SEE WHERE IT FITS
BEYOND RAZOR WIRE AND THE WALL
SOMEWHERE A PEACEFUL BLUE DOT EXISTS
IT JUST DEPENDS ON WHERE ONE SITS

THE DOOR

THEY SIT IN DIRT OUTSIDE THE DOOR
WHO? DO YOU ASK, I'LL TELL YOU WHO
THE SWOLLEN BELLIED BLANK EYED POOR

FORGOTTEN, UNSEEN, SOMBER, SORE
NO FUTURE EVER PLANNED AT ALL
THEY SIT IN DIRT OUTSIDE THE DOOR

IS IT WORTH IT TO HOPE ANYMORE?
I WONDER IF THAT'S WHAT THEY THINK
THE SWOLLEN BELLIED BLANK EYED POOR

WITH BARREN BLANKNESS TO THE CORE
NOT A SINGLE THOUGHT TO EMANATE
THEY SIT IN DIRT OUTSIDE THE DOOR

THE PAPER TREES CAME WELL BEFORE
RELATED SOME POINT IN TIME TO
THE SWOLLEN BELLIED BLANK EYED POOR

IS IT JUST? TO SPEND MORE AND MORE
WHILE MISERY MASSES IN THE MUD
THEY SIT IN DIRT OUTSIDE THE DOOR
THE SWOLLEN BELLIED BLANK EYED POOR

VILLAINESQUE

"B" HAPPEN BECAUSE I DID "A"?
THAT'S CERTAIN A QUESTION TO ASK.
DOES MY LIFE WORK THIS WAY?

WITHOUT A SCRIPT, THERE IS NO PLAY,
WHEN I FORGET MY LINES I DIE.
"B" HAPPEN BECAUSE I DID "A"?

I TOUCH THIS TWICE AND I'M OKAY,
BE SURE TO TAKE THREE, NEVER FOUR.
DOES MY LIFE ALWAYS WORK THIS WAY?

SO FAR I'VE LIVED ANOTHER DAY,
SKIPPING CRACKS AS I MOVE ALONG.
"B" HAPPEN BECAUSE I DID "A"?

GUIDED BY WHAT THE VOICES SAY,
THE UNIVERSE IS SAFE AND SOUND.
DOES MY LIFE ALWAYS WORK THIS WAY?

MAYBE NOT, BUT I HAVE TO SAY,
LOOKING UP I STILL SEE THE SKY.
"B" HAPPEN BECAUSE I DID "A"?
DOES LIFE ALWAYS WORK THIS WAY?

ANAPODOTON

In any kind of writing or speaking, *anapodoton* refers to implying a main idea by introducing a lesser idea, knowing that the main idea will be known to any listener or reader due to the commonality of the phrase. For example, if someone said, "If the shoe fits…," they would not have to say, "…wear it," because those words would be thought of automatically by the listener. A poem can use this rhetorical device to create an anapodoton poem, another type of puzzle. In the poem, "AWAY," I added the use of *anastrophe* - the inversion of the order of words normally spoken in reverse.

OY VEY

WHICH CAME FIRST
WITHOUT THE EGG THERE'D BE NO CHICK
IT'S LIKE WHICH CAUSED THE OTHER
THE ANSWER, TAKE YOUR PICK

I WAS THINKING OF THAT PARADOX
WHEN THE EMPLOYER SAID, "NOT NOW"
YOU DON'T HAVE ENOUGH EXPERIENCE
YOU'LL HAVE TO FIND IT SOMEWHERE, SOMEHOW

AND THEN I THOUGHT WHICH CAME FIRST
RELIGION OR THE PRIEST
I'M REALLY IN A QUANDARY
AND THAT'S TO SAY THE LEAST

I GUESS I'LL TRY TO GET A LOAN
TO STUDY AT SOME SCHOOL
IF THEY'LL LOAN ME WITH NO CREDIT
WHICH MIGHT BE AGAINST A RULE

IF I CAN'T GET A LOAN TO LEARN
AND JOBS VANISH IN A BLUR
I GUESS I'LL HAVE NO OPTION
BUT BECOME A PHILOSOPHER

AWAY

IF WINGS PIGS HAD
BREAKFAST LIGHT
NO SIZZLING, CURLING
IT'S AWAY IN FLIGHT

IF AWAY WAS THE CAT
SCURRYING FEET
CLEAN UP THE CRUMBS
ISN'T THAT NEAT

A DUCK IT LOOKED LIKE
THE TRIGGER I PULLED
A FRIEND IS AWAY
MISTAKE MOST CRUEL

HAIKU

A haiku has only three lines and does not rhyme. The first and last lines are each five syllables, and the second line is seven syllables. The haiku is of Japanese origin, and typically references themes of nature. Traditionally, they are written about the present, not the past or future. They are presented without titles and written in lowercase. Some modern writers have relaxed these rules and you may find some variations in theme and tense.

1.

the butterfly flies
with random scattered freedom
no destination

2.

slowly sinking sun
sets the distant trees on fire
then hides behind earth

3.

i hear the owl chirp
yet i am deaf to his flight
the silent hunter

4.

crow cries urrr urrr urrr
from the highest of branches
no reply, he flies

5.

the mountain is there
forever, behind the haze
man placed before it

6.

water can smooth rock
incidents, in time, teach man
no water, time's up

7.

wise to perch up high
the bark has hidden feathers
sundown wakes the hunt

8.

none of this is ours
mountains, water, stars
only here to share

9.

the crow pecks the tail
then hops away so quickly
the fox cannot rest

10.

there is no water
food impossible to find
men argue who's right

11.

i remove the mask
covering my mouth and nose
the others remain

12.

such beauty in flight
gooneys with massive still wings
landing, such chaos

13.

women bring forth life
while men chase devious ways
to end existence

14.

ukrainian ants
rebuild methodically
after russian rain

15.

white winter snowflakes
a christmas gift for valleys
spring sun delivers

16.

the fox is asleep
a nearby mouse finds some food
both are satisfied

17.

twisting in the grass
four paws reaching for the sun
a perfect massage

LIMERICK

A limerick follows an AABBA rhyme pattern in a single five line stanza. The subject is commonly comedic in nature. Limericks originated in the early 1800's, as a humorous drinking song, traditionally with bawdy or obscene lyrics.

THERE WAS A GUY IN NEW YORK
ATE PIZZA WITH KNIFE AND FORK
EVERYONE BOOED
THE ITALIANS ALL SUED
NOW HE JUST STICKS TO HIS PORK

IMAGINE IT RAINING IN SPAIN
NOT ON THE PLAIN BUT THE PLANE
YOU COULDN'T GET IN
UNLESS YOU COULD SWIM
YOU'RE BETTER OFF TAKING THE TRAIN

A FOOTBALLER FROM BRAZIL
PRACTICED DRIBBLING UP A STEEP HILL
IT WASN'T MUCH FUN
CAUSE GRAVITY WON
THE RACE DOWN WAS QUITE A THRILL

ONCE WAS A MAN FROM NORWAY
TOO LARGE TO FIT THROUGH A DOORWAY
ON THE DOCTOR'S CALL
THEY REMOVED A WALL
AND TRUCKED HIM RIGHT DOWN THE HIGHWAY

NOW IS WHEN I WILL WARN YA
ABOUT THE MAN FROM CALIFORNIA
WHO EATS FLOWERS LIKE GOATS
FROM ROSE PARADE FLOATS
HE'S QUITE THE GASTRIC PERFORMER

THERE WAS A MAN FROM BIG BEAR
LOST IN A BLIZZARD QUITE RARE
HIS HOUSE WAS BELOW
A MOUNTAIN OF SNOW
THE RESCUERS LOOKED EVERYWHERE

CHOKA

A choka poem is a Japanese form. It consists of alternating five and seven syllable lines, and ends with one additional seven syllable line. The total length can be any number of lines, as long as they are an odd number in total, and it ends with an additional seven syllable line. The choka form does not have a rhyming pattern.

SMOOTH PASSAGE

LEAVE YOUR BAGS BEHIND
WHEN YOU WANT TO MOVE FORWARD
IN AN EASY WAY
MEMORIES ARE GOOD AND BAD
HEAVY OR THEY'RE LIGHT
YOUR CHOICES WILL PROPEL YOU
TO KEEP ALL YOUR GOALS IN SIGHT

GIANT STEPS

WE MOVE FORWARD WHEN
A PERSON FORGETS PRUDENCE
ALLOWING PASSION
TO IGNITE VOLCANIC THOUGHTS
OTHERWISE CONTAINED
IN LONELY LIVES LIVED MUNDANE
ONE AFTER ONE ALL THE SAME

ROUNDABOUT

A roundabout has four stanzas of five lines each. Within each stanza, the second and fifth lines are identical, word for word. The third and fourth lines each contain four syllables and will rhyme with one another.

JOIN

ENJOY SOME CONVERSATION
PLEASE DON'T IRRITATE
NO SPITE NO FRIGHT
JUST SMOOTH JUST LIGHT
PLEASE DON'T IRRITATE

KONNICHIWA MY MATE
ENJOY THE MORNING'S SIGHT
LET'S RUN LET'S WALK
LET'S SIT LET'S TALK
ENJOY THE MORNING'S SIGHT

GUTEN MORGEN ES IST DIE ZEIT
BE A SOARING HAWK
FLY FREE BE ONE
PLEASE HAVE SOME FUN
BE A SOARING HAWK

BUENOS DIAS WE CAN TALK
NO MATTER OUR DISTINCTION
BE COOL NO HATE
PARTICIPATE
NO MATTER OUR DISTINCTION

TRINET

A trinet has seven lines. Lines three and four each contain six words. All other lines have two words. There are no restrictions regarding rhyme or number of syllables.

WHAT ELSE?

EARTH, WATER
FIRE, AIR
TELL ME WHAT ELSE IS THERE
TO HAVE A WELL ROUNDED LIFE
FOOD, SHELTER
LOVE, STRIFE
WHAT ELSE?

WHOEVER THEY ARE

QUESTIONS, ANSWERS
TRUTHS, LIES
ARE YOU ONE OF THOSE CONFUSED
JUST DON'T KNOW WHO TO TRUST
OR BELIEVE
FOLLOW THEM
THEY KNOW

NIGHT TIME

SHADOWY FIGURES
LURKING AROUND
RISING UP FROM UNDER THE GROUND
ENTERING MY NOSE, CHOKE MY THROAT
CAN'T BREATHE
PANIC, PANIC
WAKE UP

TRILONNET

A Trilonnet is a 14 line poem. It includes four unrhymed tercets, and one rhyming couplet. These can be either eight or ten syllables per line. Whichever you choose, all lines must be the same number.

YOU AND I

HOW IS IT WE READ THE SAME WORDS
SEE THE SAME EVIDENCE AND FACTS
INTERPRET IT ALL FAR APART

UNSTOPPABLE, IMMOVEABLE
NOTHING GOOD HAPPENS WHEN THEY MEET
JUST ENERGY EXPELLED FOR NAUGHT

HOW CAN I SEE WHAT YOU CAN SEE
HOW CAN I THINK THOSE THOUGHTS YOU HAVE
AND HOW CAN YOU DO THAT WITH ME

IMAGINE IF THERE WAS A WAY
I COULD SEE FROM BEHIND YOUR EYES
AND YOU AS WELL FROM IN MY HEAD

OUR SHARED WORLD WOULD BE FAIR WEATHER
IF OUR GOALS WERE REACHED TOGETHER

QUATRAIN

A quatrain is a four line stanza. As a style of poetry, it can be any number of stanzas in length. The rhyme pattern varies, and is typically ABAC, ABCB, or ABAB. The number of syllables per line can vary. The quatrain is derived from the French word, *quatre*, which means *four*.

MOMENTS

I SAW YOU UP AGAINST THE WALL
A WONDROUS WINDOW TO THE PAST
ANOTHER CHANCE TO SEE A MOMENT
THAT NOW I KNOW CAN NEVER LAST

SUCH A FLEETING FLASH OF FREEDOM
TO WATCH A BEING WITH NO QUEST
THINKING NOW, AND NOW, AND NOW
UNCONCERNED WITH WHAT COMES NEXT

A CHILD'S SIMPLE JOY OF LIVING
ONE LIFE, SO FULL IN EMPTINESS
A CANVAS THAT WILL FILL UP FAST
HAVING MORE TO HAVE MUCH LESS

YES, WHEN LIFE'S LESSONS WEIGHT MY HEART
AND TURN MY SPIRIT COLDER
I GAZE AT YOU AND FEEL THE WARMTH
OF THE KITTEN ON YOUR SHOULDER

OUT THERE

SITTING IN THE SAFETY OF MY ROOM,
QUIET, PEACEFUL, BLISS.
WHILE THE SUN SETS OUT MY WINDOW,
NICE TO END A DAY LIKE THIS.

THEN, A SINGLE SHAFT OF LIGHT,
COMES BEAMING IN MY VIEW,
FILLED WITH DANCING DUST.
ARE THESE PARTICLES ALL NEW?

OR WERE THEY ALWAYS THERE,
IN THE DARK UNSEEN,
MIXING WITH THE OXYGEN,
GOOD AND BAD BETWEEN.

UNTIL A LIGHT IS SHONE,
ON LIFE WE HOLD SO DEAR,
OUR QUIET, PEACEFUL, BLISS,
IS ASSUMED, BUT NOT SO CLEAR.

PLACE I HEARD OF

THERE WAS A PLACE I HEARD OF
WHERE NO ONE SAW THEIR FACE
PICTURES WERE UNHEARD OF
IN THIS VERY DIFFERENT PLACE

MIRRORS WERE A MYSTERY
AND CAMERAS NOT DESIGNED
REFLECTIVE THINGS LIKE LAKES AND STREAMS
WERE AWFULLY HARD TO FIND

AND ALL THE MEN WERE HANDSOME
AND ALL THE WOMEN PRETTY
AND ALL BECAUSE THEY THOUGHT SO
IN THIS WHAT DO I LOOK LIKE CITY

ASK YOURSELF

AM I LISTENING WHEN YOU SPEAK
OR FORMULATING MY NEXT WORD
I WISH I WASN'T SO WEAK
NOT GRASPING WHAT I HAVE HEARD

DO MY THOUGHTS HOLD MORE WEIGHT THAN YOURS
AM I LISTENING WHEN YOU SPEAK
DO MY THOUGHTS OPEN UP MORE DOORS
THAN YOURS WHICH ARE SO DIM AND BLEAK

WHEN I THINK THIS - AM I UNIQUE
OR DO WE ALL JUST ACT ALONE
AM I LISTENING WHEN YOU SPEAK
THE TRUTH MIGHT BE THAT NO ONE'S HOME

I FOCUS HARD ON WHAT YOU SAY
OF THAT I AM MY OWN CRITIQUE
BUT SADLY I FAIL EACH DAY
AM I LISTENING WHEN YOU SPEAK

SECRETS

ALL AIR WAS SILENT STANDING STILL
BENEATH A MOONGLOW LIGHT
THE WATER'S SURFACE SMOOTH AS GLASS
REFLECTING ALL IN SIGHT

NATURE'S CANVAS A SILENT LAKE
KEEPING SECRETS DOWN BELOW
BEHIND THE WONDROUS WOODED SCENE
THE SURFACE SEEMED TO SHOW

UNTIL A FISH JUMPED TO CATCH A MEAL
AND OUTWARD RIPPLES ROLLED
PERFECT CIRCLES DISTURBED THE SCENE
A CLOUD PUT THE MOON ON HOLD

NOW IN FRONT OF ME DARK WATERS
AN UNKNOWN PITCH BLACK POOL
A DARKENED DEPTH OF MYSTERY
THAT'S MADE MY SKIN GO COOL

CAN ONE MINOR MOMENT IN OUR WORLD
WAKE THE DARKNESS FROM ITS SLEEP
DO WE HAVE CONTROL OF TREMBLING SKIN
JUST BEFORE WE START TO WEEP

PAST LIVES

I WROTE THIS POEM IN THE PAST
AND HOPE TO READ IT SOMETIME IN THE FUTURE
I'M NOT SURE WHEN BUT IT WILL HAPPEN THEN
IN THAT MOMENT I WON'T TRY TO IMPROVE HER

I'LL JUST READ THE WORDS AS THEY'RE WRITTEN
THE FUTURE ONES AFTER THE PAST WORDS
THE PAST ONES BEING THOSE I'VE SPOKEN
THE FUTURE YOU HAVEN'T HEARD

WHEN I'M DONE WITH THE VERY LAST LINE
WRITING AND READING WILL BE IN THE PAST
ACCORDING TO CALENDARS, CLOCKS AND TIME
OUR LIFE IN THE PRESENT JUST CAN'T LAST

POEM IN A BOTTLE

AS THE SUN DIPS IN THE OCEAN
THE HORIZON GLOWS IN RED
TOMORROW WILL FOR SURE DELIGHT
THAT'S WHAT THE SAILORS SAID

I'M SADDENED WHEN I THINK OF THEM
THE STORM WAS JUST TOO STRONG
I DON'T KNOW HOW I MADE IT HERE
TO LIVE WHO KNOWS HOW LONG

I FOUND A STREAM FOR WATER
PLUS COCONUTS HYDRATE
SEAWEED HAS BEEN NOURISHING
AND MANGOES DO TASTE GREAT

SPELLED HELP IN THE SAND AT LEAST TEN TIMES
USING MANY ROCKS AND SHELLS
BUILT SMOKY FIRES EVERY DAY
FOR NAUGHT; A DOT AMONGST THE SWELLS

I DON'T KNOW WHAT'S HAPPENING
IN A WORLD THAT'S DISAPPEARED
FOR YEARS I THOUGHT I CARED
NOW FINDING ME IS WHAT I'VE FEARED

WITH MY FINAL SHRED OF PAPER
AND THIS PEN THAT'S ALMOST DONE
I LAUNCH A POEM IN A BOTTLE
FROM PARADISE, DON'T COME

180 DEGREES

PASSING PYRAMIDS OF POLISHED FRUIT
MELONS STACKED AND BERRIES BOXED
ALL CONVENIENT, THREE FEET OFF THE FLOOR
A MOTHER WANDERS THROUGH A STORE

CONDITIONED AIR FEELS SO NICE
KEEPS LETTUCE CRISP AND CARROTS FRESH
ONE ROOM DEDICATED FOR GREENS AND MORE
A MOTHER WANDERS THROUGH A STORE

PACKAGED GOODS ON MANY SHELVES
CASHEWS, PEANUTS, PISTACHIOS
DRIED FRUITS AND BEANS GALORE
A MOTHER WANDERS THROUGH A STORE

FROZEN FARE FROM EVERYWHERE
FISH, MEAT, PASTA AND DESSERTS
SHIPPED BY PLANE, TRUCKED TO THE DOOR
A MOTHER WANDERS THROUGH A STORE

DOWN DAIRY AISLES ARE MILKS AND CHEESE
SO MANY KINDS TO CHOOSE
HOW COULD SHOPPING EVER BE A BORE
A MOTHER WANDERS THROUGH A STORE

IN A SOMALI DESERT EYES PEER THROUGH FLIES
AT DRIED UP CROPS AND SUN SCORCHED EARTH
A MOTHER WANDERS KNOWING WHAT'S IN STORE
HER HUNGRY CHILD SOON TO BE NO MORE

*TO HELP, GOOGLE UNITED NATIONS WORLD FOOD PROGRAM

DON'T WORRY, BE HAPPY

MOST OF US APPEAR HAPPY MOST OF THE TIME
SWIMMING UPSTREAM IN A WORLD OF GLOOM
FIGHTING HARD TO IGNORE THE SIGNS
OF THE APPROACHING IMPENDING DOOM

ONE HALF OF ALL GUNS THAT EXIST IN THE WORLD
ARE LOCATED LOCAL IN A USA ROOM
READY TO FIRE IF AN INVECTIVE IS HURLED
WHAT A LIFE OF IMPENDING DOOM

SOME WOMEN LIVE LIFE UNDER A THUMB
NOT A HAPPY HOME THIS TOMB
LIVING HIS WISHES TO WARD OFF HIS FISTS
A LIFE OF IMPENDING DOOM

DEREGULATION HELPED THE TRAIN GO OFF
EXPLODING IN A TOXIC FUME
A WHOLE TOWN LEFT WITH A RASH AND A COUGH
LIVING WITH IMPENDING DOOM

WE WORKED AND LEARNED A LOT ON ZOOM
WHILE A VIRUS LOCKED US AWAY
NOW WE LIVE WITH EVER IMPENDING DOOM
AWAITING THE REPLICANT TO RETURN SOME DAY

DECONFLICTION PHONES RINGING AGAIN
WE ALL THINK OF THE SKYWARD MUSHROOM
THE END COULD OCCUR WITH ONE SIMPLE MISTAKE
WE'RE LIVING WITH IMPENDING DOOM

IT DOESN'T MATTER WHERE YOU ARE
UNLESS FLOATING IN A WARM WOMB
THE WORLD IS JUST A DANGEROUS PLACE
A SPHERE OF IMPENDING DOOM

SAVANNAH

SAVANNAH CAME INTO THIS WORLD
OF IRON, BRICK AND STONE
TWO YEARS AGO TO THIS DAY
SHE WAS HAPPY IN HER HOME

THEN ONE DAY THE FAMILY LEFT
MOM, DAD, SIS AND HER
HURTLING DOWN A HIGHWAY
A MESMERIZING BLUR

HER SISTER GEORGIA WAS MUCH OLDER
UNDERSTOOD THE ARDUOUS RIDE
TO VISIT THAT MOST MAGICAL PLACE
THAT WALT HAD SET ASIDE

GEORGIA COULDN'T SLEEP AT ALL
SHE WATCHED THE CITY TURN TO TREES
WHILE SAVANNAH SLEPT IN A SAFETY SEAT
HER BLANKY ON HER KNEES

PART WAY THERE SAVANNAH WOKE
HER MOTHER TOOK HER HAND
SAVANNAH GAZED AT NEON SIGNS
WAS THIS THAT MAGIC LAND

THEY WALKED INTO THE WAFFLE HOUSE
GOT A TABLE IN THE BACK
SAVANNAH HAD A SPECIAL SEAT
BEING READIED FOR HER SNACK

HER EYES SCANNED ACROSS THE ROOM
AND STOPPED WHEN SHE SAW THE MAN
TWO TABLES OVER HE SAT ALONE
STROKING HIS BEARD WITH A MASSIVE HAND

SAVANNAH BOLTED TOWARD THE MAN
HER ARMS SAID, "LIFT ME PLEASE"
HIS EXPRESSION SAID, "WHAT DO I DO"
AS SAVANNAH HUGGED HIS KNEES

HER PARENTS SAID THEY'RE SORRY
TRIED TO PRY THE GIRL AWAY
SAVANNAH HELD ON TIGHTER
AS THE ROOM WAS HELD AT BAY

...

THE MAN SAID, "I GOT THIS"
AS HE PICKED SAVANNAH UP
HE ROCKED HER GENTLY IN HIS ARMS
AND SANG MY LITTLE DIXIE CUP

EVERYONE STOOD AND CLAPPED THEIR HANDS
NOT KNOWING WHAT THEY'D SEEN
BUT SOMEHOW FEELING DEEP INSIDE
SOMETHING'S SPECIAL IN THIS SCENE

SAVANNAH REACHED FOR HER DAD
HE GENTLY TOOK HER IN HIS ARMS
SHE GRABBED HIS NECK AND PULLED HIM CLOSE
AS IF TO SAY THERE WAS NO HARM

LIFE IS FULL OF MYSTERIES
IN THE FUTURE AND THE PAST
HOLD ON WHEN THEY COME YOUR WAY
THEY DISAPPEAR SO FAST

WHO'S RIGHT

MORE AND MORE PEOPLE
BREATHING OUT MORE CO_2
LESS AND LESS TREES CONVERT
AHEAD WHAT WILL WE DO

LIKE OBLIVIOUS FISH IN A TINY BOWL
WE'RE POLLUTING OUR OWN WORLD
NO ADULT TO CHANGE THE WATER
ALL BUSY FIGHTING FOR FLAGS UNFURLED

USING UP OUR RESOURCES
AS FAST AS WE POSSIBLY CAN
PUTTING OFF CONSEQUENCES
TO A FUTURE TIME WHEN

RATHER THAN FIGHT OVER FLAGS UNFURLED
WE CAN ARGUE WHO'S TO BLAME
FOR LIVING LIFE IN MISERY
THOUGHTLESS FISH IN A BOWL OF SHAME

POEM FROM A NEIGHBORING GALAXY
(TRANSLATED TO ENGLISH)

THE DOMINANT SPECIES IS HUMAN
AT LEAST THAT'S WHAT WE THINK
BECAUSE ALL THE OTHER SPECIES
WILL SOON BECOME EXTINCT

THEY DON'T ALL LOOK OR SPEAK THE SAME
THEY'RE SHORT, TALL, DARK, AND LIGHT
THE MAIN COMMONALITY
IS THEY ALWAYS SEEM TO FIGHT

THOSE THAT LOOK LIKE THIS
HATE THOSE THAT LOOK LIKE THAT
AND THOSE THAT LOOK LIKE THAT
ACT LIKE AN ARISTOCRAT

THE THESE AND THOSE DON'T AGREE ON LOVE
IT'S THEIR WAY OR ELSE IT'S WRONG
TWO HUMANS CAN FEEL THE MUSIC
BUT THEIR SOCIETY WRITES THE SONG

EVEN THOSE WHO SHARE THE SAME LAND
ARGUE, DISAGREE, AND ACT RUDE
AND ALL BECAUSE OF ONE SIMPLE FACT
THEIR LOCATION IN THE LATITUDE

A THIRD OF THAT WORLD BELIEVE IN THE WRONG GOD
SAY THE HALF THAT BELIEVE IN SOME OTHER
THE BALANCE BELIEVE THERE'S NO GOD AT ALL
IT'S CHAOTIC AT BEST WE DISCOVER

OF COURSE THE MAJORITY WILL KILL THEMSELVES OFF
WE NEED ONLY WORRY ABOUT THE HANDFUL THAT ROAM
YEARS FROM NOW THEY'LL HAVE A FEW ROCKETS
TO START SEARCHING FOR THEIR NEW HOME

SOME KIDS

SOME KIDS WANT TO BE DIFFERENT
SO THEY CUT HOLES IN THEIR CLOTHES
THEY SPRAY THEIR HAIR TIL IT STANDS UP STRAIGHT
AND PUT EARRINGS IN THEIR NOSE

AND THEN THEY STAND BY A CANDY STORE
AND MAKE UP COOL NICKNAMES
AND STAND AROUND, AND STAND AROUND
ALL DIFFERENTLY THE SAME

TRUE FREEDOM

A BIRD UP ABOVE LOOKING DOWN AT ME
I WONDER IF HE IS AWARE
HE'S MUCH BETTER OFF BEING FREE
OF BOUNDARIES, RULES AND HISTORY

I'VE NEVER SEEN AN EMACIATED CROW
THEY ALL SEEM TO DO JUST FINE
GLIDING AND SOARING THEY PUT ON A SHOW
STARVING NEVER STOPPING THEIR FANCIFUL FLOW

A BIRD NEVER FLIES INTO A WALL WITH INTENT
BECAUSE LIFE ISN'T PROCEEDING SO WELL
I BET THAT THOUGHT NEVER CAME OR WENT
IMAGINE LIFE WITHOUT TORTURING TORMENT

CUTTING THROUGH THE SILENCE THAT EXISTS UP HIGH
ABOVE MAN'S CACOPHONOUS BUSTLE
THE SILENT CATHEDRAL OF OPEN VAST SKY
ALLOWS WONDROUS FLIERS TO CATCH MY STILL EYE

IF ONLY I COULD SPREAD MY WINGS
CATCH AN UPDRAFT FROM A MOUNTAINSIDE
DIVE AND RISE AND DO ALL THEIR THINGS
AND EXPERIENCE WHAT TRUE FREEDOM BRINGS

STAMPEDE DREAMS

WE RUMBLED IN SLOW MOTION
MY BUFFALO BROTHERS AND I
TOWARDS DISTANT DARK STORM CLOUDS
ROILING IN A SHIMMERING SKY

A DRIP OF DARKNESS ZIGZAGGED DOWN
FROM THE CENTER OF A FOAMING CLOUD
LIKE A SWIRLING CROOKED POINTER
AN OMINOUS MARKER FOR OUR CROWD

IT POINTED TO A STAND OF TREES
ALONE IN THE DISTANT DUST
THEIR GNARLY BRANCHES SPELLING "EDGE"
WAS THIS A FACT TO TRUST

THE THOUGHT OCCURRED IN MY MIND
I REALLY SHOULD GET OUT NOW
BUT SHOULDER TO SHOULDER THIS MASS WAS ONE
I JUST COULDN'T FIGURE OUT HOW

IF I COULD POSSIBLY TURN AROUND
THOUSANDS OF EYES WOULD GLARE AT ME
EACH ONE SHOUTING *TRAITOR*
FOR ALL THE WORLD TO SEE

BUT NOT GIVING UP ON A BAD IDEA
IS A WORSE IDEA AT BEST
WE'LL KNOW FOR SURE AS WE PILE UP
AND OUR MOVEMENT COMES TO REST

HATS

WHITE HATS AND BLACK HATS
WE ALL OWN A FEW
THEY'RE READY TO WEAR
EACH MOMENT THAT'S NEW

WE ALL GET TO CHOOSE
TO PICK THE RIGHT ONE
TO SHOW HOW WE THINK
AND WHAT WE'VE BECOME

FOR ALL OF OUR LIVES
WE DRESS OUR OWN STYLE
SOMETIMES LOOKING GOOD
THEN BAD FOR AWHILE

WHITE HATS AND BLACK HATS
WE ALL OWN A FEW
THE CHOICE IS ALL OURS
WHICH ONE IS FOR YOU

HAPPY

WHY IS HAPPINESS SO ELUSIVE
ALWAYS AROUND THE NEXT BEND
MAYBE ONE MORE VACATION
SURELY ONE MORE FRIEND

WHEN I GET MY FINANCES FIXED
AND SUMMER COMES AROUND
I'LL HAVE REASON TO BE SMILING
MANY GOOD TIMES WILL ABOUND

I'LL GATHER EVERYTHING I NEED
TO HAVE A HAPPY WORLD
JUST LIKE I DID THE YEAR BEFORE
WHEN TROUBLE ROUND ME SWIRLED

BUT WHAT IF HAPPY WASN'T HARD
AND EXISTED JUST BECAUSE
JUST BECAUSE I SAID SO
EVEN WITH MY MANY FLAWS

IF ONLY I COULD REALLY GET
BEING HAPPY STARTS WITH ME
I'D REALLY NEED NO REASONS
I'D BE HAPPY AS CAN BE

TANDEM REGRESSION

I HAVE THE POWER TO RESIST
WEAR MY BLINDERS EVERY DAY
DEFLECT, DENY, DEFILE, DECRY
OH YOU KNOW I WILL PERSIST

I'LL HAVE MY PRIVATE POINT OF VIEW
OBTAINED FROM OBSCURITY
A POINT OF VIEW QUITE DUBIOUS
BUT FOR NOW WILL HAVE TO DO

MY POWER MAKES ME POWERFUL
AT LEAST IN MY MIND'S EYE
I PUT STICKS IN SPOKES REPEATEDLY
IN A CHINA SHOP I AM THE BULL

THE MORE YOU TRY TO THWART ME
THE MORE I'LL IGNITE THE FLAMES
I'M IGNITED BY YOUR INSISTENCE
THAT I'M A FOOL WHO DOESN'T SEE

I HAVE THIS POWER TO RESIST
FUELED BY DISTRUST AND DISLIKE
I'M BY YOUR SIDE FOREVER
TOGETHER WE'LL PERSIST

NINE

I DON'T WANT TO BE A SIGN IN A WINDOW
FADING IN THE SIZZLING SUN
ONLY TO BE REPLACED
BY A SIMILAR SILENT ONE

I DON'T WANT TO BE A USELESS LADDER
THAT HAS NO RUNGS TO CLIMB
OR A BELL WITHOUT A CLAPPER
SO STILL WITHOUT A CHIME

I WANT TO LIVE AND LEARN
DISCOVER KNOWLEDGE AND TO BE
AN ASSET TO THE WORLD
A BETTER PART OF HISTORY

I WANT TO MAKE A DIFFERENCE
CONTRIBUTE TO THE GROUP
I'M JUST NOT SURE I WILL SURVIVE
WHEN THERE'S CHEMICALS IN MY SOUP

EXHAUSTIVE JOURNEY

WHEN YOU ROLL THESE DICE
THERE'S A LIFE COULD BE LOST
IN A MYSTERIOUS SYSTEM
THAT CAN'T COUNT THE COST

A FIVE YEAR OLD FEARED FOOTSTEPS
A SIX YEAR OLD A BELT
WHEN THE LIGHT GETS LIT IN THE HALL
FEAR IS WHAT THEY FELT

THERE IS A REPORT OF ABUSE
BUT STILL THEY TREMBLE THERE
AWAITING A RANDOM RULING
HOPING SOMEONE WILL PLEASE CARE

THEN THERE'S FEAR OF COURTS
JUDGES DECIDE THEIR FATE
THERE'S FEAR OF RETURN TO A HOME
OF UNACCOUNTABLE HATE

THEY MIGHT GO TO A RELATIVE
OR A RESIDENTIAL HOME
OR JOIN A FOSTER FAMILY
FOR NOW, JUST A LOAN

BECAUSE THE COURTS MUST REVIEW
IS THIS A FINAL CHOICE
UNFORTUNATE FOR KIDS
THEY REALLY HAVE NO VOICE

EVEN IF THEY STAY IN FOSTER CARE
WHEN SOON THEY TURN EIGHTEEN
IF THEY AREN'T SOON ADOPTED
THEY'RE BACK AT THEIR CRIME SCENE

ONCE AGAIN, WHEN YOU ROLL THESE DICE
THERE'S A LIFE THAT COULD BE LOST
IN A MURKY MYSTERIOUS SYSTEM
THAT CANNOT COUNT THE COST

THE FREEDOM ROOM

ANGRY MEN SHOOT BULLETS
POLITICIANS TAKE A STAND
MORE GUNS ARE WHAT WE NEED
TO PROTECT US IN THIS LAND

ANGRY MEN DO IT AGAIN
KIDS BLEEDING ON THE FLOOR
ARM THE TEACHERS SAY OUR LEADERS
WE NEED GUNS SO MUCH MORE

ANGRY MEN DO IT AGAIN
SHOPPERS LYING DEAD
SECURITY IS ON THE FLOOR
BULLETS IN THEIR HEAD

STORES AND MALLS ARE CLOSING
EVERYONE'S HOME SCHOOLED
EVERYTHING COMES FROM AMAZON
STRAY BULLETS ROUND HERE RULE

BUT IF EVERYONE WAS ARMED
THEY COULD TAKE THESE MADMEN OUT
PANICKED BULLETS FLYING EVERYWHERE
A SOLUTION THAT I DOUBT

EVENTUALLY FEAR WILL WIN
WE'LL ALL HIDE INSIDE
PISTOL ON THE TABLE
WHILE OUR FREEDOM IS DENIED

AI

THE GREATEST APP IS ON MY PHONE
YOU HAVE TO GIVE IT A TRY
IT CAN TALK FOR HOURS ON AND ON
IT'S MY PERSONAL AI

FORGET SLICED BREAD, PAPER CLIPS
ESCALATORS AND EV'S
THE COOLEST ITEM EVER
IS AI YOU'LL CLEARLY SEE

WHEN A SALESMAN'S AT MY DOOR
AND I DON'T REALLY WANT TO BUY
I SAY JUST WAIT A MINUTE
PATCH HIM IN TO MY AI

WHEN UNCLE JOE CALLS AND BRAGS
HIS GRANDSON'S S.A.T. WAS HIGH
AND M.I.T. IS CALLING SOON
I PATCH HIM IN TO MY AI

ON THOSE EXHAUSTIVE LONG VACATION DRIVES
WHEN SONNY ASKS ABOUT THE SKY
WHY IS IT SO BLUE DADDY
PATCH HIM IN TO YOUR AI

NOW I FEEL SO RELAXED AND CALM
AVOIDING TALKING ALL THE TIME
WITH MY PERSONAL AI
MY BRAIN'S A SOOTHING SILENT CHIME

SAFE

COMFORTABLE IN THE SHALLOW END
WE ALL APPEAR QUITE BORED
WE WONDER WHY DAYS BLEND TO ONE
WHY THERE'S JUST NO VISION FORWARD

WE SPLASH AROUND AND IT LOOKS LIKE FUN
NOT LIKE A RESCUE REQUIRED
EVEN THOUGH THE WATER'S PURE
IT KEEPS US FIRMLY MIRED

CONVINCED THIS IS WHERE WE OUGHT TO BE
TOGETHER AND ALL ALONE
WITH TOMORROW BEING YESTERDAY
AND TODAY NOT AT ALL UNKNOWN

NEVER LIKING CHANGE AT ALL
UPSET WHEN LIFE ISN'T THE SAME
TOTALLY IN CONTROL OF CHOICE
HAVING NO ONE ELSE TO BLAME

PRONOUN RIDERS

HE WHO KNOWS WHO HOW AND WHY
LIVES IN A BUBBLE OF TRUST
CREATED CONTROLLED AND CONCOCTED
BY THOSE WHO THINK ANSWERS A MUST

THEY WHO KNOW WHO HOW AND WHY
HAVE THEIR OWN VERSION OF COURSE
WE'RE ALL MOVING SIDEWAYS SLOWLY
RIDING A TWO-HEADED HORSE

WE'LL NEVER CONVINCE EACH OTHER
OUR WAY IS FACTUALLY RIGHT
SO LET'S PRETEND WE'RE BOTH CORRECT
AS WE SAY OUR PRAYERS GOOD NIGHT

LIFE DREAMING

I THINK THEREFORE I AM
THINK ABOUT THAT FOR AWHILE
ALL THAT I SEE, THAT I HEAR, THAT I TOUCH
EVIDENCE I NEATLY COMPILE

I MULLED IT OVER TO PROVE I EXIST
AND I ALMOST HAD SETTLED THAT
BUT WHAT IF I HAD NO LANGUAGE
WITH NO DISCUSSION DOES THE LINE GO FLAT?

OF COURSE NOT I BOLDLY THINK
A BABE WITH NO LANGUAGE EXISTS
WITH NO INNER VOICE TO CONSTANTLY ASSURE
I AM, I AM, I'M QUITE SURE OF THIS

YET AS I ASSEMBLE THESE THOUGHTS ALONE
I STILL WONDER IF ALL IS A DREAM
WHOSE DREAM I REALLY CAN'T SAY
COULD IT BE YOURS AND MINE WITH NO IN BETWEEN

PERFECT WORLD

I RUN ACROSS THE GRASS
DESTINATION IS UNKNOWN
THAT WILL BE FOR LATER
WHEN I'M FULLY GROWN

I FOCUS LIKE A BUTTERFLY
FIRST I'M HERE THEN THERE
MY PURPOSE IS NO PURPOSE
JUST EXISTING LIKE THE AIR

I SCREAM AND SOMETIMES SHOUT
WITH EXUBERANCE AND JOY
THE WORLD TO ME IS PERFECT
I'M THREE AND JUST A BOY

PERENNIAL

ENERGY'S NOT CREATED
AND NEVER IS DESTROYED
IT DEPENDS ON WHERE IT IS
AND HOW IT IS DEPLOYED

WHEN THIS TURN IS OVER
I'D LIKE TO HAVE A CHOICE
TO CHOOSE THE NEXT ADVENTURE
AT LEAST TO HAVE A VOICE

I WANT TO LIVE IN WARMTH
SURROUNDED BY MY FRIENDS
SLEEP AWAY THE WINTERS
HAVE A LIFE THAT NEVER ENDS

SPRING TO LIFE IN APRIL
SWAY IN SUMMER'S BREEZE
BE A SOURCE OF JOY
OF COMFORT AND OF EASE

TWO WHISPERS

THE SCENT WAS DELIGHTFUL
THE PRESENCE MADE IT CLEAR
MORE WAS TO FOLLOW
THE WHISPER IN THE EAR

ANTICIPATION HOVERS
TREMBLING IS CLEAR
WHAT WILL HAPPEN AFTER
A WHISPER IN THE EAR

AND THEN THERE WAS A TIME
YOUR WORLD FILLED WITH FEAR
ALL BECAUSE YOUR SECRET
WAS WHISPERED IN YOUR EAR

EVERY FACE IS MOCKING
TO YOU IT SEEMS QUITE CLEAR
A LIFE TURNED UPSIDE DOWN
FROM A WHISPER IN AN EAR

DEVIL'S BLOOD

THE NIGHT WIND HOWLED
THE BARN DOOR CRASHED
UNDER THE HAY
MY LIQUOR STASHED

IT WAS AGED IN A BARREL
FOR A WEEK OR TWO
NOT ACTUALLY GOOD
BUT IT'D HAVE TO DO

THE YOUNG BOYS WERE COMING
FOR FRIDAY NIGHT TALES
SIT ROUND THE FIRE
HEAR ME REGALE

BUT THIS NIGHT WAS DIFFERENT
THE BOYS SAT WAY BACK
EXCEPT FOR BRAVE BILLY
UP FRONT DRESSED IN BLACK

I TOLD EVERY STORY
I THOUGHT I WAS DONE
BILLY SAID, "ANOTHER,
YOU KNOW THE ONE,

THE ONE YOU NEVER TELL
THE ONE YOU KEEP HIDDEN
THE REASON FOR WHISKEY
THE ONE THAT'S FORBIDDEN"

THE TEARS STARTED FLOWING
DOWN MY CRACKED SKIN
A SHUTTER FLEW OPEN
A COLD WIND BLEW IN

THE BOYS JUMPED UP
RAN FOR THE DOOR
BILLY MOVED CLOSER
SAID, "TELL ME SOME MORE"

MY MIND STARTED SPINNIN'
THINKING OF ELLY MAE
HOW WE FOUGHT BY THE RIVER
THAT SAD AWFUL DAY

...

IF I HADN'T BEEN DRINKING
THAT DEVIL'S BLOOD
SHE WOULDN'T HAVE LAIN THERE
SO STILL IN THE MUD

I CRASHED MY WALKING STICK
DOWN ON THE HAY
SENDING THE KILLER
DRAINING AWAY

BILLY JUMPED UP
HIGH AS A KITE
RAN FOR HIS LIFE
WAS SOON OUT OF SIGHT

I NEVER SAW BILLY
AFTER THAT DAY
WE BOTH MADE A CHOICE
TO RUN FAR AWAY

FIRSTS

TODAY'S A DAY OF FIRSTS
FIRST DAY ON THE LINE
FIRST DAY AT THE FRONT
WHERE KILLING'S NOT A CRIME

FIRST DAY BEING FAR FROM HOME
TODAY'S A DAY OF FIRSTS
FIRST DAY BEING TWENTY-ONE
WHILE BOMBS AROUND YOU BURST

TODAY YOUR WIFE HAD YOUR SON
FIRST CHILD FOR YOU BOTH
TODAY'S A DAY OF FIRSTS
AS YOU FULFILL YOUR OATH

YOU COULDN'T SEE THE SHELL ARRIVE
NOW WILL BEGIN THE WORST
THE LAST DAY OF YOUR LIFE
TODAY'S A DAY OF FIRSTS

SPARK

LIKE A MIGHTY CITY
THE FOREST HAS IT ALL
ELDERLY TREES THAT HAVE SEEN THE YEARS
SAPLINGS NOT YET TALL

SEASONS COME AND GO
SEEDS FALL AND ARE REBORN
EVERY VIBRANT LIFE SHARING
FROM THE CORNUCOPIA HORN

THESE TREES HAVE NO ARROGANCE
TO BE BETTER THAN THEIR NEIGHBORS
ONLY CITIES HAVE THE HUMANS
WITH THEIR NEED TO BE CRUSADERS

WITH RECKLESS SELFISH ACTIONS
FECKLESS FEARS AROUSE A FOMENT
MEEK MINDS GET INFILTRATED
ALL IS POISED FOR THAT MOMENT

WHEN A SPARK IGNITES A ROAR OF FLAMES
SOON THERE'S NOTHING LEFT TO SAVE
A BARREN BURNED OUT WASTELAND
HUMAN HATRED DUG THE GRAVES

DEFINITIONS DEFINED

WHAT IS A METAPHOR?
IT'S FOR USING WORDS THAT DON'T BELONG
BUT STILL CONVEY THE STORY
STILL ILLUMINATE THE SONG

THIS MAY SEEM QUITE ABSTRACT
TO NOT SAY WHAT YOU REALLY MEAN
AND HOPE THAT ALL THE READERS
SEE THE MEANINGS IN BETWEEN

SWITCH

THEY'RE MOVING FORWARD SLOWLY
SILENT SUICIDAL ROWS
THE ICON'S PROXIES QUIET
AS THE GRASS BENEATH THEIR TOES

GREEN TURNS BROWN AND BARES THE EARTH
FOR TEARDROPS FROM THE SKIES
THAT RINSE MAN'S BLOOD TO THE GROUND
BLOODY MUD UP TO THEIR THIGHS

LONG CORRIDORS IN THE GROUND
HAD A PURPOSE TO PROTECT
YES THAT WAS THE THOUGHT IN MIND
WAY BEFORE THE FAMILIES WEPT

AND SO WERE HOLES LIKE FOXES DUG
THAT BROUGHT DEATH DOWN DEEPER YET
FOR THOSE POOR SACRIFICIAL MEN
FREE CHIPS FOR A RISKY BET

THOSE ICONS STAND SIX FEET UP
SOLDIERS LIE SIX FEET DOWN
WOULD IT ALWAYS BE THIS WAY
IF THE OTHER WAY AROUND

SHARE

BEFORE YOU LEAVE
SHOW YOUR HAND
FOR ALL TO SEE
AND UNDERSTAND

THIS PIECE OF YOU
YOU LEAVE BEHIND
JUST MIGHT HELP
SOMEONE UNWIND

THEN ALL BEFORE
WOULD BE WORTHWHILE
YOU WOULDN'T BE
A GHOST ON TRIAL

IF EVERYTHING
WORKS OUT THAT WAY
YOUR HEAD'S HELD HIGH
AT END OF DAY

SO THAT YOU WON'T
BE SO PERPLEXED
WHEN YOU MOVE ON
TO SEE WHAT'S NEXT

REMINDER

AN UNSEEN LOCOMOTIVE
SCREAMED ACROSS OUR LAWN
HIT THE HOUSE, SHOOK THE WALLS
FOR A MOMENT, THEN WAS GONE

I SAT IN SILENT DISBELIEF
WATCHING WATER WAVING IN MY GLASS
WONDERING WHAT THE HELL WAS THAT
AND IF IT HAD NOW PASSED

IT WASN'T ME IMAGINING
THE DOG AND CAT BOTH FROZE
BOTH OF THEM FRAUGHT WITH FEAR
FROM THE PHANTOM NO ONE KNOWS

THAT ROSE UP FROM THE DARKEST DEPTHS
TO REMIND US ONCE AGAIN
WE'RE NOT THE ONES MOST POWERFUL
IN FACT, WE'RE NOTHING NOW AND THEN

THREE SQUIRRELS

WHILE GAZING THROUGH MY WINDOW
FROM THE COMFORT OF MY CHAIR
I WATCHED THREE SQUIRRELS IN A TREE
HIGH UP IN THE AIR

THEY DARTED LEFT, DARTED RIGHT
PLAYING TAG ON SKINNY BRANCHES
I WONDERED IF THEY THOUGHT AT ALL
ABOUT TAKING RISKY CHANCES

HEART OF GOLD

EVERYONE SAID SHE HAD A HEART OF GOLD
SO WHEN THE CROWDS OF MEN CAME ROUND
THEY BROUGHT THEIR PICKS AND AXES
TO DIG INTO HER SOUL

PERHAPS SHE WAS A PEACH YOU KNOW
BEING SWEET AND SOFT AND RIPE
THE MEN LOOKED FOR A WAY TO BITE
INDIFFERENT TO HER GLOW

THE RESTLESS WOLFPACK WAITED
WITH SLICK HAIR AND SMILING FACES
FOR THE TIME TO MAKE A MANLY MOVE
AND FINALLY BE ELATED

THEY NEVER GAVE HER ANY CHANCE
TO PARTICIPATE AT ALL
THEIR MODUS OPERANDI WAS
THIS SELFISH, SINFUL DANCE

LUCKILY HER WEALTH WAS SAFE
SHE RECOGNIZED THE PREY
SAID, "SORRY BOYS," AND WALKED AWAY
I'M NOT A WEAKENED WAIF

CURIOSITY

I TRIED TO WRITE SOME POETRY
WHILE HIGH ON THC
BUT ALL I DID WAS EAT LOTS OF CHIPS
AND GO ON A LAUGHING SPREE

AND COCAINE DIDN'T HELP AT ALL
MY THOUGHTS CAME WAY TOO FAST
COULDN'T KEEP UP WITH MY PEN
THERE WAS NOTHING I COULD GRASP

THEN I TRIED SOME LSD
CAUSE ALLEN DID IT TOO
BUT I GOT STUCK IN A METAPHOR
SAN FRANCISCO IN A SHOE

HEROIN WAS NEXT TO TRY
BUT SOON I NODDED OUT
LAID MY CHEEK ON PAPER
MY AWAKENING WAS IN DOUBT

AND FINALLY SOME FENTANYL
SEEMS LIKE THE ONE THAT
HAS ME WRITE MY FINAL LINE
CURIOSITY KILLED THE

SELF-ISH GAMES

WHAT A WONDERFUL GAME
WITH SELF ON THE SIDELINE
OBSERVING THE WINS AND LOSSES
COACHING US FROM TIME TO TIME

THE MIND MAKES MOST DECISIONS
BELIEVES TO BE ACTING ALONE
BUT CREATION COMES FROM NOTHING
MAYBE A NUDGE FROM THE SELF AT HOME

THE SELF IS PRIMARILY OBSERVER
ENJOYING EACH NEW RIDE
TWEAKING THINGS HERE AND THERE
SUBTLY FROM INSIDE

EVENTUALLY GAMES ALL END
THE FIELD MAY BE SILENT AND STILL
BUT ENERGY FLOWS ALL AROUND
AND TRAVELS WHERE IT WILL

OH HI

IN YELLOW SPRINGS MARY KNOWS ELIJAH
HELLO IS RINGING UP AND DOWN THE STREET
WHEN JOSE NEEDED A FEW HELPING HANDS
HE COULD COUNT ON FRANK AND PETE

WHEN ABRAHAM HAD A BIRTHDAY
CHEYENNE BROUGHT THE CAKE
SVETLANA CAME WITH ISABEL
AND JADEN CAME WITH JAKE

ROMAN DANCED WITH IVAN
SERENITY KISSED PIERRE
MALIK SANG WITH PEDRO
AND NO ONE SEEMED TO CARE

THE MANTRA HERE IS LET'S BE FRIENDS
FOR SUSAN, DESTINY, JOE AND JACK
MOHAMED, ALICIA, CALEB AND JIM
ALL CHOOSE TO NEVER GO BACK

GO BACK TO SELFISH SINGLE-MINDED RULES
NEVER RETURN TO ME FIRST NOT YOU
NOT HERE WHERE PEOPLE MEET AND GREET
OH HI, OH HI, OH HOW DO YOU DO

HOW TO VOTE

I DON'T WANT TO BE MISINFORMED
I WANT TO BE SMART OF COURSE
I'LL WATCH THE PRETTY LADY ON TV
SHE SEEMS A RELIABLE SOURCE

AND THEN THERE'S ALWAYS UNCLE NED
THE LOUDEST VOICE IN THE ROOM
HE MUST BE RIGHT TO BE SO CERTAIN
ALL OTHER OPINIONS ARE DOOMED

I GUESS MY FAVORITE ACTOR OR ACTRESS
COULD ALWAYS LEND A HAND
I THINK I COULD GET SOME GOOD ANSWERS
FROM MY FAVORITE MUSICAL BAND

I'M SURE WHEN I'M READY TO CAST MY VOTE
I WILL CERTAINLY CONSIDER THEM ALL
OR MAYBE I'LL BE A LOT MORE ACCURATE
WITH MY GRANDSON'S MAGIC EIGHT BALL

BEING

SILENT STREAMS OF AUTUMN SUN,
PIERCE THE CRISP CHILL AIR,
WARMING ROSY CHEEKS,
OF A CHILD WHO'S LYING THERE.

QUIETLY, IN A BED OF LEAVES,
HER EYES SO GENTLY CLOSED,
BEING WITH THE PEACEFULNESS,
THAT NATURE OFTEN SHOWS.

A BURST OF WIND MAKES COLORED LEAVES,
DANCE ACROSS THE LAWN,
CREATING SOOTHING SOUNDS,
AS THEY WHIRL AND SWIRL ALONG.

ARMOR

EACH PATCH OF INK SLIPPED BENEATH THE SKIN
BECOMES PART OF THE TORTOISE SHELL
PROVIDING A PRIVATE HIDING PLACE
FROM PERILOUS POINTS OF HELL

EACH SHINY SILVER STUD AND CHAIN
PRISON BARS BEFORE THE FACE
DO THEIR BEST IN THE HUMAN PLAY
TO COVER BUT NOT ERASE

LIKE GLADIATORS ARMORED UP
TO PROTECT THEIR REAL THIN SKIN
THE ACCOUTREMENTS ARE BARRIERS
FROM THE LIONS DEEP WITHIN

THE ARENA CROWDS FILL EVERY DAY
HOLDING THUMBS UP OR DOWN
ARE YOU IMMUNE IN YOUR PRIVATE CELL
PROUDLY WEARING YOUR TRANSLUCENT CROWN

BARELY HERE

A BEAR CAME DOWN THE TRAIL
PAST EVERGREENS AND SHALE
PAST BERRY BUSH AND SQUIRRELS
PAST WRINKLED WIND BLOWN MAIL

ANCIENT ROCKS PAINTED OVER
SMOKE PACKS WITH CELLOPHANE
PAST CRUSHED CANS AND STRAWS
SADDENED HERE HE CAME

WHEN THE FOREST DISAPPEARED
A SUBDIVISION CAME IN VIEW
WITH BLACKENED TRAILS AND FISHLESS LAKES
A BEAR COULD NOT UNDO

HE TURNED AND RAN UPHILL
FLEEING FROM THE BLIGHT
THEY PUT ME ON THEIR FLAG
THEN THEY RUN ME OUT OF SIGHT

SOMETHING ELSE TO WORRY ABOUT

I FORGOT TO BREATHE TODAY
I DON'T KNOW FOR HOW LONG
I DON'T THINK I SHOULD WORRY
BUT I MIGHT BE VERY WRONG

I FORGOT TO BREATHE TODAY
AND YET I'M STILL ALIVE
WHAT IF I FORGET AGAIN
AND THEN I DON'T SURVIVE

HAND AND EYE

IN A DIMLY LIT SPACE
HER EYES AND HAND WERE ONE
ROLLING INK ON PAPER
UNTIL THE IMAGE COMES

A DARK FOREBODING FIGURE
STANDS WHEN SHE IS DONE
A WONDROUS WORK OF ART
YES, HER EYES AND HAND WERE ONE

THE POND

IN AFRICA THE BAD GUYS WEAR WHITE HATS
VIETNAMESE CALLED IT THE AMERICAN WAR
BOTH SIDES OF CONGRESS USE IMMIGRATION
AS A TOOL TO KEEP THEIR FEET ON THE FLOOR

WHEN A SHOPLIFTER GETS PUNCHED IN THE FACE
THE COPS ARREST THE OWNER OF THE STORE
WHO THEN GETS SUED BY THE THIEF
THE OWNER OWNS THE STORE NO MORE

PERSPECTIVE PERSPECTIVE PERSPECTIVE
EVERY ISLAND IS A MOUNTAINTOP
EVERY WORD YOU SPEAK IS A RIPPLE
IN A POND OF PERSPECTIVE SLOP

THE BOAT

FIVE ON PORT WANT TO ROW EAST
WHILE FIVE ON STARBOARD CHOOSE WEST
THEY CAN'T AGREE SO PORT ROWS ALONE
WHILE STARBOARD TAKES A REST

THEN THEY SWITCH AND STARBOARD ROWS
WHILE PORT STUBBORNLY SITS AND POUTS
A LOT OF ENERGY IS WASTED AWAY
WHILE THE BOAT DOES SOME ROUNDABOUTS

MOMENT TO MEMORY

EACH MOMENT IS A MEMORY
WAY TOO NUMEROUS TO RECLAIM
NOT EASILY ACCESSIBLE
FROM OUR SCATTERED, CLUTTERED BRAIN

EACH OLD MEMORY STARTED NEW
EITHER RANDOM OR CREATED
AND STAYS OR GOES AT OUR CONTROL
HIDDEN DEEP OR SIMPLY STATED

LOSING WINNERS

THE EARTH CHOSE TO BE THE EARTH
AND THE SEA THE SEA
THEY EACH WIN FIRST PRIZE
FOR BEING WHAT THEY BE

THE MOON CHOSE TO BE THE MOON
THE SUN THE SUN
SOME PEOPLE CHOOSE TO HAVE NO LIFE
IN LOSING THEY HAVE WON

EQUIVOCATE

THE RIDICULOSITY OF THE STATEMENTS
SUCH GROSS MISUNDERSTATEMENT
A HODGEPODGE OF VERBILAGE
FOR THE FOLLOWIST, THE PATIENT

WITH RESEARCH RELAXADAISICAL
HISTORY DIMLY REMEMORABLE
THE CREATIVENESS TO INDEPENDENIZE
PROPELS IDEAS SO CLICKABLE

STILL FLYING

A MONARCH WITH CRUSHED WING
SO LUCKY TO MEET MY WIFE
WHO FED HIM HONEY WATER
THAT ADDED DAYS TO HIS LIFE

HE CLUNG TIGHT TO HER FINGER
HUNG UPSIDE DOWN IN HIS CAGE
DRANK FROM WATERMELON CUBES
ENJOYED HIS GOLDEN AGE

SO SAD WHEN THE MORNING CAME
THAT HIS BODY LIE FLAT AND STILL
WHILE HIS PEACEFUL RANDOM SPIRIT
FLEW BEYOND A SNOWY HILL

ALL OF YOUR HEART

LOVE YOUR CHILD WITH ALL OF YOUR HEART
PASS FORWARD KNOWLEDGE WHILE YOU CAN
STUFF OF KINDNESS, OF LOVE TO START
KNOWLEDGE IS NOT JUST ABOUT STEM

HER FUTURE FILLED WITH SMILING FRIENDS
LOVE YOUR CHILD WITH ALL OF YOUR HEART
SUPPORTING HER DREAMS NEVER ENDS
DAY ONE TIL THE DAY YOU DEPART

HE WON'T BE ALONE IF YOU'RE SMART
IF HIS FOUNDATION'S SOLID, STRONG
LOVE YOUR CHILD WITH ALL OF YOUR HEART
AND YOU WILL HAVE DONE NOTHING WRONG

THEN LOVE OTHERS LIKE YOUR OWN CHILD
MAKE THE WORLD BOTH LIGHTER AND SMART
SO FOR THEM THE WORLD'S NOT SO WILD
LOVE YOUR CHILD WITH ALL OF YOUR HEART

RHYMING COUPLET

A rhyming couplet consists of two lines of similar length and meter that rhyme with one another. These two lines will typically work together to complete the same thought. Rhyming couplets were very popular in Shakespeare's works and can make up poems of any length.

WHO

WHO DESIGNS THE WAY YOU WALK
WHOSE WORDS COME OUT WHEN YOU TALK

WHO'S AT FAULT WHEN THINGS GO WRONG
WHO MAKES YOUR DAY WEAK OR STRONG

WHOSE DAY IS SAD AND WHO'S TO BLAME
WHO'S HAVING FUN; WHO CHOSE THE GAME

WHO'S THE HEART OF WHO YOU ARE
WHO STOPS NOW; WHO TAKES YOU FAR

WHO DECIDES WHAT YOU CAN BE
YOU? COULD IT BE; COULD IT BE

THE GIFT

IN THE LONELY NIGHT OF THE TWENTY FIFTH
I OPENED A MYSTIC MYSTERY GIFT

I DON'T KNOW FROM WHAT SECRET SOURCE IT CAME
APPEARED UPON MY PORCH WITHOUT A NAME

TURNS OUT TO BE A CANVAS THREE BY TWO
WITH ASSORTED PAINT AND EASEL TOO

STARK WHITE AND BLANK LIKE WINDOW VIEWS OF SNOW
WHAT IS THERE I COULD PAINT? I JUST DON'T KNOW

I NEED AN INSPIRATION TO BEGIN
THERE ARE NONE IN THIS FROZEN WORLD I'M IN

TWO MONTHS PASS AT LEAST AND SHE'S STILL WHITE
STARING AT ME, DARING ME TO TAKE FLIGHT

THEN ABOVE THE SNOW COLOR IS DISPLAYED
A BRIGHTLY COLORED PETAL NATURE MADE

ONE GIFT HAD ME FIND ANOTHER I KNOW
A FLOWER PUSHING THROUGH A CRUST OF SNOW

EVERYONE

IF EVERYONE WERE JUST LIKE YOU
IN SPEECH, IN THOUGHT, IN THE WAY THEY GREW

SAME EYES, SAME TEETH, SAME HAIR, SAME NOSE
SAME COLOR, SHAPE, SAME TASTE IN CLOTHES

IF EVERYONE WERE JUST LIKE YOU
AND LIKED THE SAME THINGS THAT YOU DO

AND HAD THE SAME TEN FAVORITE SONGS
AND KNEW THE SAME IDEAS WERE WRONG

AND ONLY LIKED ONE KIND OF BOOK
ONE KIND OF GAME, ONE KIND OF COOK

AND WISHED THE WISH YOU'RE WISHING FOR
AND DREAMED YOUR DREAM FROM THE NIGHT BEFORE

IF EVERYONE WERE JUST LIKE YOU
OH, HOW BORING; ONE POINT OF VIEW

HOLIDAY HAPPINESS

ARM IN ARM AROUND THE BABY GRAND
A REUNITED FAMILY STANDS

ELATED, WARMED, BY THE TIME OF YEAR,
THEY SING THOSE SONGS THAT THEY HOLD SO DEAR

SLEIGH BELLS AND MANGERS, REINDEER AND STARS,
SONGS THAT REMIND US JUST WHO WE ARE

THIS SPECIAL MOMENT, TIME FOR A TEAR,
OF JOY, OF LOVE, AND THOUGHTS OF NEXT YEAR,

WHEN ONCE AGAIN, HERE WE WILL STAND,
ARM IN ARM AROUND THE BABY GRAND

ACKNOWLEDGEMENT

I began writing in high school and honestly can't remember if there was a reason why - an encouraging person or some inspiration. I was not prolific in any way. After high school, I went into the service and had many hours between engine room shifts on an aircraft carrier to read and write. My writing picked up during this period, and my mother would neatly rewrite and save anything I sent her. After the service, I went blank for years as I worked and started a business. When I married and had kids, an idea came to me for a unique Christmas gift for my children. I would create poems specific to my child's activities. I would then write them out on adding machine paper and roll them up backwards in a ball, which then continued to be rolled up in different colored streamer paper with coins and trinkets rolled into the mix here and there. It was always a big hit for them to unroll, find trinkets and coins, and read the poems. Years later, my wife Arlene encouraged me to sign up for college writing courses at a local university. I did, and thoroughly enjoyed all three classes I took. From these classes came my first published book and many other poems and short stories. One professor who especially inspired me was Roger Goodwin. Again, there was a dry spell for years when other priorities took over. After retiring, I was encouraged by my wife to sign up for a poetry club at the local senior center. We meet once a month and read what we have written during the previous four weeks, usually following a prompt to use a certain style or subject (like *scary* for Halloween). I have been awakened again by this group and write more now than ever in my life.

I have to credit my mother, my children Eric and Jaimie, my wife Arlene, Professor Roger Goodwin, and the Rancho Cucamonga Senior Poetry Club.

Printed in Great Britain
by Amazon